# STUDY GUIDE

## A World Divided: Superpower Relations, 1943-72

Edexcel - IGCSE

# CLEVER Lili

Published by Clever Lili Limited.

contact@cleverlili.com

First published 2020

ISBN 978-1-913887-05-6

Copyright notice

All rights reserved. No part of this publication may be reproduced in any form or by any means (including photocopying or storing it in any medium by electronic means and whether or not transiently or incidentally to some other use of this publication) with the written permission of the copyright owner. Applications for the copyright owner's written permission should be addressed to the publisher.

Clever Lili has made every effort to contact copyright holders for permission for the use of copyright material. We will be happy, upon notification, to rectify any errors or omissions and include any appropriate rectifications in future editions.

Cover by: Misu on Adobe Stock

Icons by: flaticon and freepik

Contributors: Lynn Harkin, Petia Hak

Edited by Paul Connolly and Rebecca Parsley

Design by Evgeni Veskov and Will Fox

All rights reserved

# DISCOVER MORE OF OUR IGCSE HISTORY STUDY GUIDES
*GCSEHistory.com and Clever Lili*

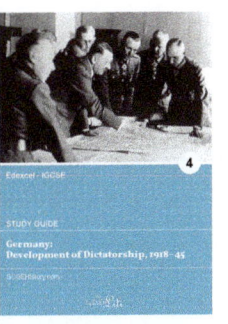

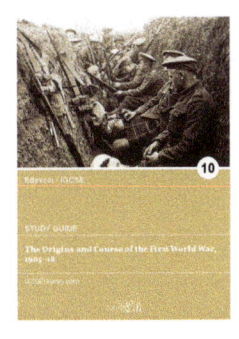

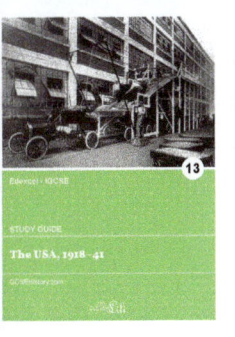

- 4 — Edexcel IGCSE Study Guide: Germany: Development of Dictatorship, 1918–45
- 8 — Edexcel IGCSE Study Guide: Russia and the Soviet Union, 1905–24
- 9 — Edexcel IGCSE Study Guide: Dictatorship and Conflict in the USSR, 1924–53
- 10 — Edexcel IGCSE Study Guide: The Origins and Course of the First World War, 1905–18
- 11 — Edexcel IGCSE Study Guide: The Vietnam Conflict, 1945–75
- 12 — Edexcel IGCSE Study Guide: A Divided Union: Civil Rights in the USA, 1945–74
- 13 — Edexcel IGCSE Study Guide: The USA, 1918–41
- 16 — Edexcel IGCSE Study Guide: Changes in Medicine, c1848–c1948
- 40 — Edexcel IGCSE Study Guide: China: Conflict, Crisis and Change, 1900–89

## THE GUIDES ARE EVEN BETTER WITH OUR GCSE/IGCSE HISTORY WEBSITE APP AND MOBILE APP

GCSE History is a text and voice web and mobile app that allows you to easily revise for your GCSE/IGCSE exams wherever you are - it's like having your own personal GCSE history tutor. Whether you're at home or on the bus, GCSE History provides you with thousands of convenient bite-sized facts to help you pass your exams with flying colours. We cover all topics - with more than 120,000 questions - across the Edexcel, AQA and CIE exam boards.

GCSEHistory.com — GET IT ON Google Play — Download on the App Store

# Contents

How to use this book .................................................................. 5
What is this book about? ............................................................ 6
Revision suggestions .................................................................. 8

## Timelines
A World Divided: Superpower Relations, 1943-72 ........................ 12

## Origins of the Cold War
Cold War Introduction and Definition ........................................ 14
Russian Revolution .................................................................. 15
Russian Civil War .................................................................... 16
Grand Alliance ........................................................................ 18
Tehran Conference, 1943 .......................................................... 19
Yalta Conference, Feb 1945 ...................................................... 20
Potsdam Conference, July 1945 ................................................ 22
The Atomic Bomb .................................................................... 23
The Long Telegram, 1946 ........................................................ 24
The Novikov Telegram, 1946 .................................................... 25
Satellite States, 1946-49 .......................................................... 25
Iron Curtain Speech, 1946 ........................................................ 26
Truman Doctrine, 1947 ............................................................ 27
Marshall Plan, 1947 ................................................................ 28
Cominform, 1947 .................................................................... 29
Comecon, 1949 ...................................................................... 30

## The Berlin Crisis, 1948 to 1949
Berlin Blockade, 1948-49 ........................................................ 31
Berlin Airlift, 1948-49 ............................................................ 32
Two Germanies ...................................................................... 33

## The Military Response
NATO, 1949 .......................................................................... 34
Warsaw Pact, 1955 ................................................................ 35
Arms Race ............................................................................ 36

## The Cold War in the 1950s
The Korean War ...................................................................... 37
The Invasion of South Korea .................................................... 41
USA's Involvement with the Korean War .................................... 42
General MacArthur and the Korean War .................................... 43
Impact of the Korean War ........................................................ 44
Peaceful Coexistence .............................................................. 45
De-Stalinisation ...................................................................... 46
Hungarian Uprising, 1956 ........................................................ 47

## The Berlin Crisis, 1958 to 1961
Berlin Crisis, 1958-61 .............................................................. 49

The Berlin Wall, 1961-62 ........................................................ 50

## The Cuban Crisis, 1959 to 1962
Cuban Revolution, 1959 .......................................................... 51
U2 Crisis ................................................................................ 52
Bay of Pigs, 1961 .................................................................... 53
Cuban Missile Crisis, October 1962 .......................................... 54

## The Czechoslovakian Crisis, 1968
Prague Spring, 1968 ................................................................ 56
Dubček .................................................................................. 58
Brezhnev Doctrine, 1968 ........................................................ 59

## The Thaw and Early Détente, 1963 to 1972
Détente .................................................................................. 60
China and Détente .................................................................. 61
Hotline, 1963 .......................................................................... 62
Test Ban Treaty, 1963 .............................................................. 63
Outer Space Treaty, 1967 ........................................................ 64
Nuclear Non-Proliferation Treaty, 1968 .................................... 64
SALT 1, 1972 .......................................................................... 65
Prime Minister Attlee .............................................................. 66
Fulgencio Batista .................................................................... 66
Leonid Brezhnev .................................................................... 67
President Jimmy Carter .......................................................... 67
Prime Minister Churchill .......................................................... 68
President Eisenhower .............................................................. 68
George Kennan ...................................................................... 69
President John F Kennedy ........................................................ 70
Nikita Khrushchev .................................................................. 71
George Marshall .................................................................... 72
Imre Nagy .............................................................................. 72
Nikolai Novikov ...................................................................... 73
Antonin Novotný .................................................................... 73
President Roosevelt ................................................................ 73
President Harry Truman .......................................................... 74

Glossary ................................................................................ 75
Index ...................................................................................... 79

*Quizzes, amazing exam preparation tools and more at GCSEHistory.com*

# HOW TO USE THIS BOOK

In this study guide, you will see a series of icons, highlighted words and page references. The key below will help you quickly establish what these mean and where to go for more information.

## Icons

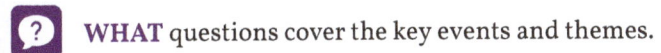

**WHAT** questions cover the key events and themes.

**WHO** questions cover the key people involved.

**WHEN** questions cover the timings of key events.

**WHERE** questions cover the locations of key moments.

**WHY** questions cover the reasons behind key events.

**HOW** questions take a closer look at the way in which events, situations and trends occur.

**IMPORTANCE** questions take a closer look at the significance of events, situations, and recurrent trends and themes.

**DECISIONS** questions take a closer look at choices made at events and situations during this era.

## Highlighted words

**Abdicate** - occasionally, you will see certain words highlighted within an answer. This means that, if you need it, you'll find an explanation of the word or phrase in the glossary which starts on **page 75**.

## Page references

**Tudor** *(p.7)* - occasionally, a certain subject within an answer is covered in more depth on a different page. If you'd like to learn more about it, you can go directly to the page indicated.

*Get our free app at GCSEHistory.com*

# WHAT IS THIS BOOK ABOUT?

A world divided: superpower relations, 1943-72 is the period study that investigates the origins of the Cold War, three of the key Cold War Crises and the attempts to ease the tensions of the Cold War. You will study the role key individuals played during the Cold War, as well as how the Cold War impacted specific countries. You will focus on crucial events during this period, and study the different political, economic and military changes that occurred.

## Purpose
This study will help you to understand the complexities of the Cold War. You will investigate themes such as communism, capitalism, sphere of influence, satellite states, containment and the arms race. This course will enable you to develop the historical skills of identifying key features of a time period, and encourages you to analyse and compare sources and evaluate interpretations.

## Topics
A world divided: superpower relations, 1943-72 is split into 5 enquiries:

- Enquiry 1 looks at the origins of the Cold War and why it occurred. You will investigate the long-term conflict between the superpowers. You will study the collapse of the Grand Alliance and its impact on Europe.
- Enquiry 2 looks at the early years of the Cold War conflict from 1945 to 1959. You will investigate how tension mounted over the future of Germany and how the divisions between the USSR and the USA deepened politically, economically and militarily.
- Enquiry 3 looks at the development of the Cold War in the 1950s. You will study the impact of the Korean War and the arms race on the relationship between the US and the USSR. You will investigate why the Hungarian Uprising occurred, the key events and its impact.
- Enquiry 4 looks at the three key Cold War crises. You will study the Berlin Crisis of 1958 to 1961, the Cuban Missile Crisis and the Czechoslovakian Crisis of 1968. For each case study, you will investigate the causes, the main events and the consequences of the crisis on international relations.
- Enquiry 5 looks at the period of Détente. You will study how and why the superpowers moved towards easing of tension between 1963 and 1972. You will investigate key events such as the introduction of a hotline after the Cuban Missile Crisis, and SALT 1. You will study the reasons for détente and how it had developed by 1972.

## Key Individuals
Some of the key individuals studied on this course include:

- President Roosevelt.
- Prime Minister Churchill.
- Premier Stalin.
- President Truman.
- Premier Khrushchev.
- Premier Brezhnev.
- Fidel Castro.
- President John F Kennedy.

## Key Events
Some of the key events you will study on this course include:

- The three wartime conferences.
- The Soviet takeover of eastern Europe.
- The Berlin Blockade and Airlift.
- The Arms Race.
- The Cuban Missile Crisis.
- The Prague Spring.
- Détente.

## Assessment
A world divided: superpower relations, 1943-72 forms part of paper 1 where you have a total of 1 hour and 30 minutes to complete. You should spend 45 minutes on this section of the paper. There will be 1 exam question on A world divided:

# WHAT IS THIS BOOK ABOUT?

superpower relations, 1943-72. The question will be broken down into 4 sections; a, b, c(i) and c(ii). You will answer a, b and either c(i) or c(ii).

- Question a is worth 6 marks. This question will require you to examine an extract and assesses your ability to analyse and evaluate a historical interpretation. You will need to identify the author's opinion or perspective by analysing the language the author uses and what they have chosen to comment on. You will explain how valid the overall impression is by using your own knowledge to evaluate that impression.

- Question b is worth 8 marks. This question will require you to explain two effects of an event on something else by using your contextual knowledge and looking at the consequences. You will need to identify two effects and then demonstrate how the event led to the effect you have identified.

- Question c(i) and c(ii) are worth 16 marks. This question will require you to construct an argument to support and challenge an interpretation stated in the question. You will be given two pieces of information to help jog your memory but you must use information of your own. You will have the opportunity to show your ability to explain and analyse historical events using 2nd order concepts such as causation, consequence, change, continuity, similarity and difference.

# REVISION SUGGESTIONS

**Revision!** A dreaded word. Everyone knows it's coming, everyone knows how much it helps with your exam performance, and everyone struggles to get started! We know you want to do the best you can in your IGCSEs, but schools aren't always clear on the best way to revise. This can leave students wondering:

- ✔ How should I plan my revision time?
- ✔ How can I beat procrastination?
- ✔ What methods should I use? Flash cards? Re-reading my notes? Highlighting?

Luckily, you no longer need to guess at the answers. Education researchers have looked at all the available revision studies, and the jury is in. They've come up with some key pointers on the best ways to revise, as well as some thoughts on popular revision methods that aren't so helpful. The next few pages will help you understand what we know about the best revision methods.

## How can I beat procrastination?

This is an age-old question, and it applies to adults as well! Have a look at our top three tips below.

### Reward yourself

When we think a task we have to do is going to be boring, hard or uncomfortable, we often put if off and do something more 'fun' instead. But we often don't really enjoy the 'fun' activity because we feel guilty about avoiding what we should be doing. Instead, get your work done and promise yourself a reward after you complete it. Whatever treat you choose will seem all the sweeter, and you'll feel proud for doing something you found difficult. Just do it!

### Just do it!

We tend to procrastinate when we think the task we have to do is going to be difficult or dull. The funny thing is, the most uncomfortable part is usually making ourselves sit down and start it in the first place. Once you begin, it's usually not nearly as bad as you anticipated.

### Pomodoro technique

The pomodoro technique helps you trick your brain by telling it you only have to focus for a short time. Set a timer for 20 minutes and focus that whole period on your revision. Turn off your phone, clear your desk, and work. At the end of the 20 minutes, you get to take a break for five. Then, do another 20 minutes. You'll usually find your rhythm and it becomes easier to carry on because it's only for a short, defined chunk of time.

## Spaced practice

We tend to arrange our revision into big blocks. For example, you might tell yourself: "This week I'll do all my revision for the Cold War, then next week I'll do the Medicine Through Time unit."

*Quizzes, amazing exam preparation tools and more at GCSEHistory.com*

## REVISION SUGGESTIONS

This is called **massed practice**, because all revision for a single topic is done as one big mass.

But there's a better way! Try **spaced practice** instead. Instead of putting all revision sessions for one topic into a single block, space them out. See the example below for how it works.

This means planning ahead, rather than leaving revision to the last minute - but the evidence strongly suggests it's worth it. You'll remember much more from your revision if you use **spaced practice** rather than organising it into big blocks. Whichever method you choose, though, remember to reward yourself with breaks.

### Spaced practice (more effective):

| week 1 | week 2 | week 3 | week 4 |
|---|---|---|---|
| Topic 1 | Topic 1 | Topic 1 | Topic 1 |
| Topic 2 | Topic 2 | Topic 2 | Topic 2 |
| Topic 3 | Topic 3 | Topic 3 | Topic 3 |
| Topic 4 | Topic 4 | Topic 4 | Topic 4 |

### Massed practice (less effective)

| week 1 | week 2 | week 3 | week 4 |
|---|---|---|---|
| Topic 1 | Topic 2 | Topic 3 | Topic 4 |

Get our free app at GCSEHistory.com

## REVISION SUGGESTIONS

### What methods should I use to revise?

**Self-testing/flash cards**

**Self explanation/mind-mapping**

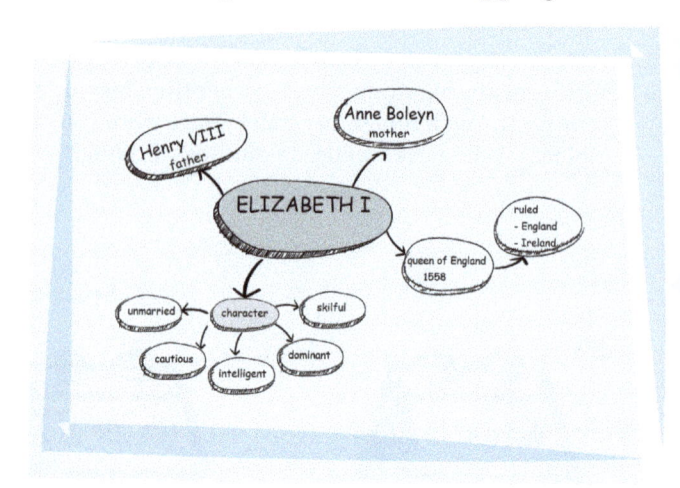

The research shows a clear winner for revision methods - **self-testing**. A good way to do this is with **flash cards**. Flash cards are really useful for helping you recall short – but important – pieces of information, like names and dates.

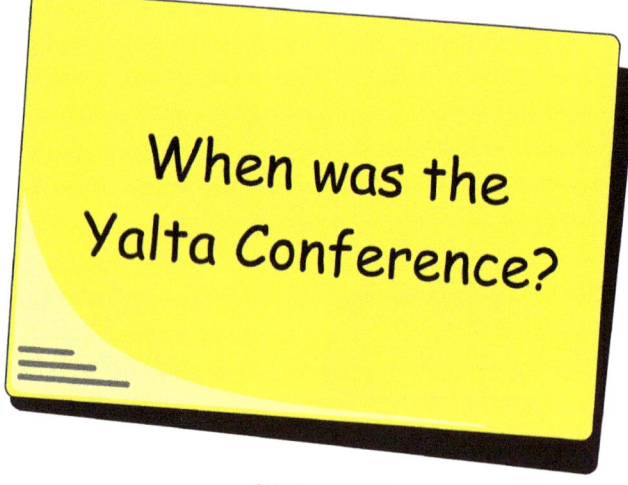

Side A - question

Side B - answer

Write questions on one side of the cards, and the answers on the back. This makes answering the questions and then testing yourself easy. Put all the cards you get right in a pile to one side, and only repeat the test with the ones you got wrong - this will force you to work on your weaker areas.

pile with right answers

pile with wrong answers

As this book has a quiz question structure itself, you can use it for this technique.

Another good revision method is **self-explanation**. This is where you explain how and why one piece of information from your course linked with another piece.

This can be done with **mind-maps**, where you draw the links and then write explanations for how they connect. For example, President Truman is connected with anti-communism because of the Truman Doctrine.

*Quizzes, amazing exam preparation tools and more at GCSEHistory.com*

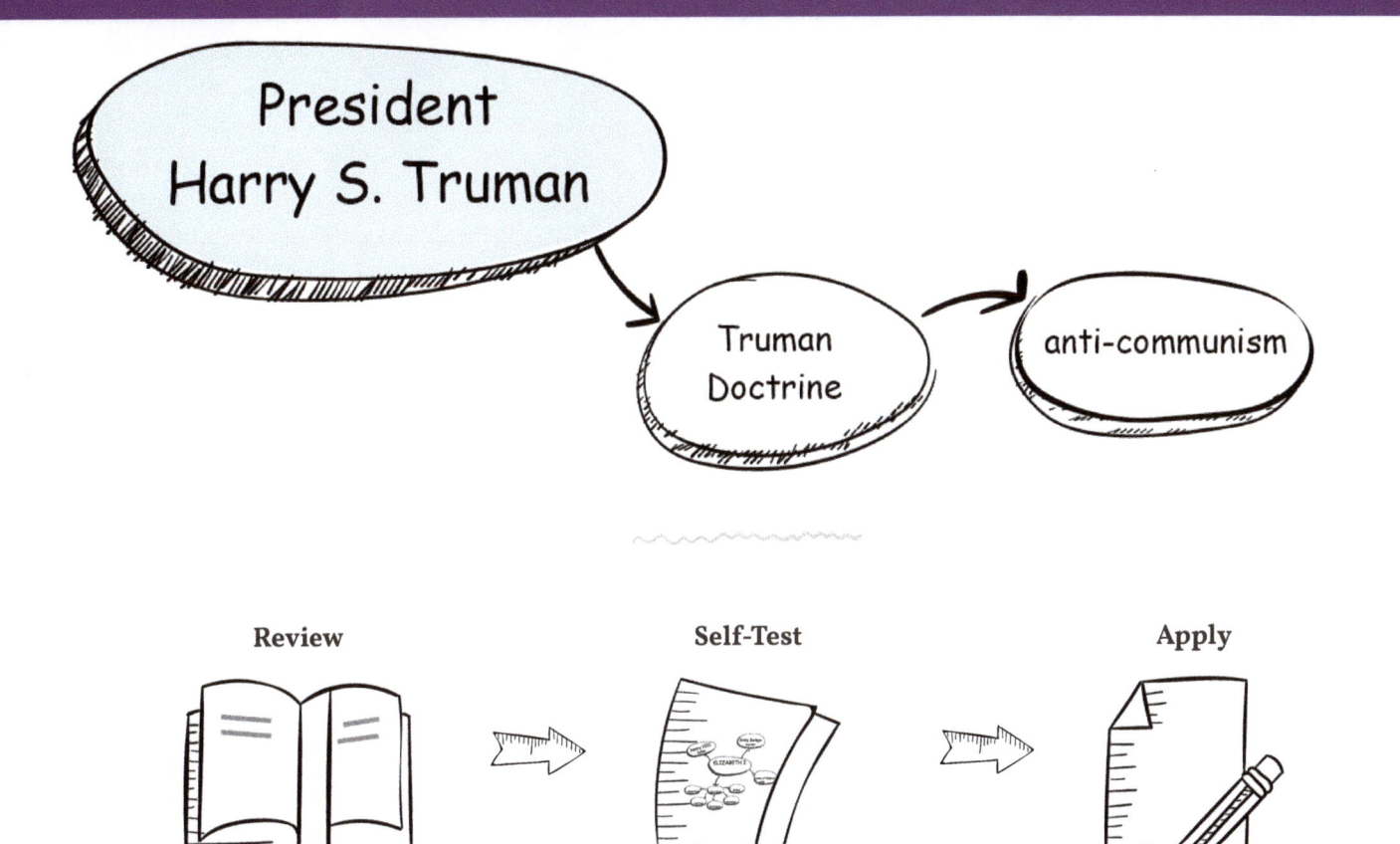

## REVISION SUGGESTIONS

President Harry S. Truman → Truman Doctrine → anti-communism

**Review**

Start by highlighting or re-reading to create your flashcards for self-testing.

**Self-Test**

Test yourself with flash cards. Make mind maps to explain the concepts.

**Apply**

Apply your knowledge on practice exam questions.

### Which revision techniques should I be cautious about?

**Highlighting** and **re-reading** are not necessarily bad strategies - but the research does say they're less effective than flash cards and mind-maps.

**Highlighting**

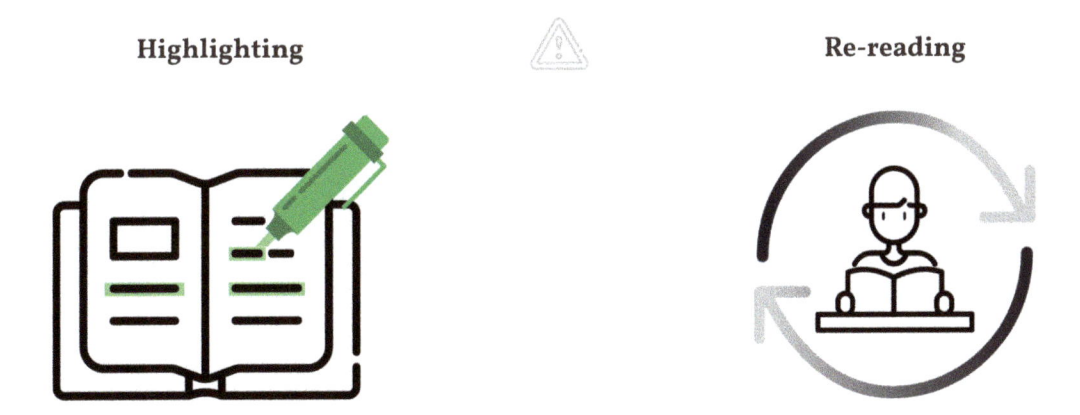

**Re-reading**

If you do use these methods, make sure they are **the first step to creating flash cards**. Really engage with the material as you go, rather than switching to autopilot.

*Get our free app at GCSEHistory.com*

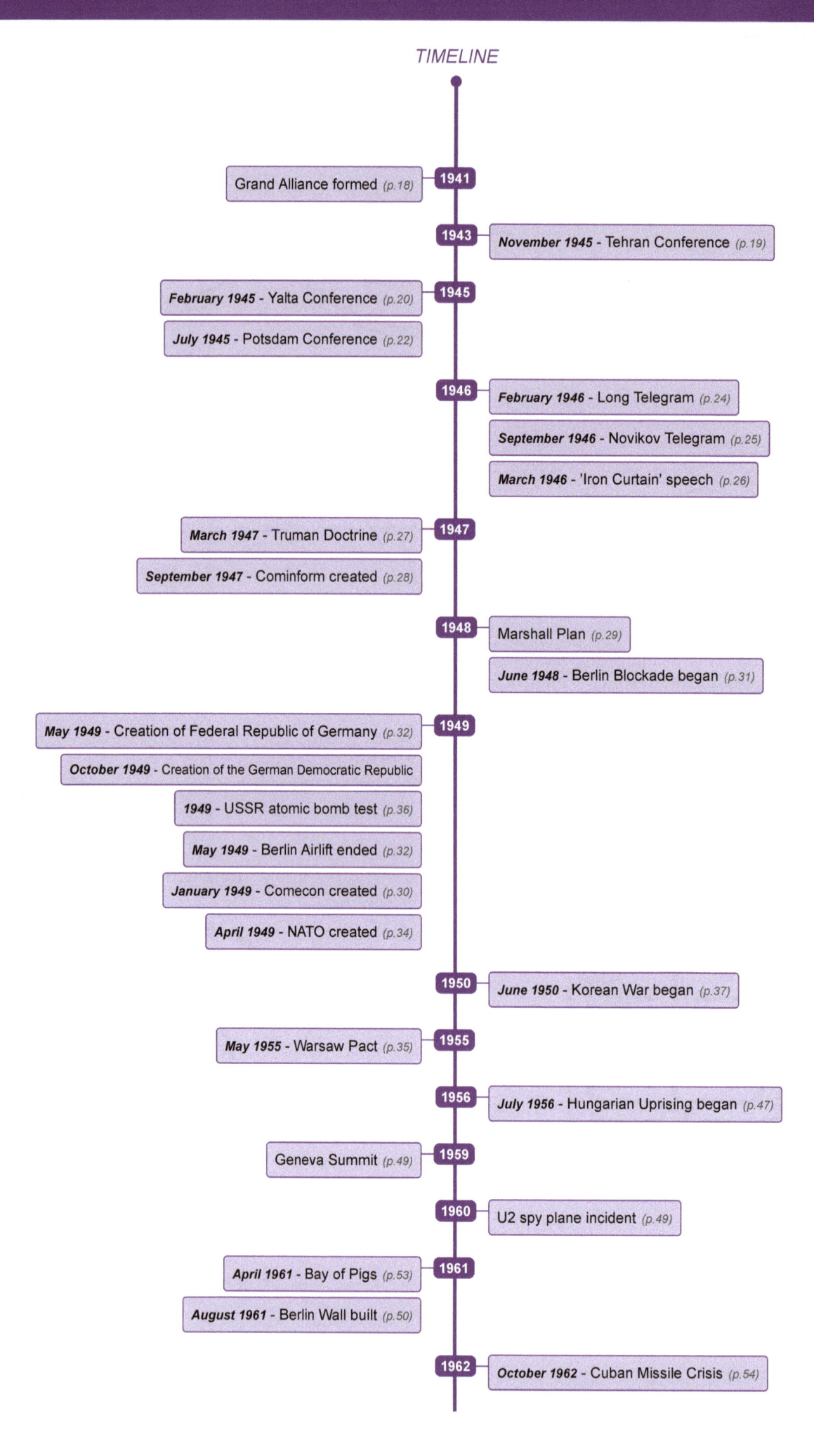

# A WORLD DIVIDED: SUPERPOWER RELATIONS, 1943-72

*TIMELINE*

- **1941** — Grand Alliance formed *(p.18)*
- **1943** — *November 1945* - Tehran Conference *(p.19)*
- **1945**
  - *February 1945* - Yalta Conference *(p.20)*
  - *July 1945* - Potsdam Conference *(p.22)*
- **1946**
  - *February 1946* - Long Telegram *(p.24)*
  - *September 1946* - Novikov Telegram *(p.25)*
  - *March 1946* - 'Iron Curtain' speech *(p.26)*
- **1947**
  - *March 1947* - Truman Doctrine *(p.27)*
  - *September 1947* - Cominform created *(p.28)*
- **1948**
  - Marshall Plan *(p.29)*
  - *June 1948* - Berlin Blockade began *(p.31)*
- **1949**
  - *May 1949* - Creation of Federal Republic of Germany *(p.32)*
  - *October 1949* - Creation of the German Democratic Republic
  - *1949* - USSR atomic bomb test *(p.36)*
  - *May 1949* - Berlin Airlift ended *(p.32)*
  - *January 1949* - Comecon created *(p.30)*
  - *April 1949* - NATO created *(p.34)*
- **1950** — *June 1950* - Korean War began *(p.37)*
- **1955** — *May 1955* - Warsaw Pact *(p.35)*
- **1956** — *July 1956* - Hungarian Uprising began *(p.47)*
- **1959** — Geneva Summit *(p.49)*
- **1960** — U2 spy plane incident *(p.49)*
- **1961**
  - *April 1961* - Bay of Pigs *(p.53)*
  - *August 1961* - Berlin Wall built *(p.50)*
- **1962** — *October 1962* - Cuban Missile Crisis *(p.54)*

*Quizzes, amazing exam preparation tools and more at GCSEHistory.com*

# A WORLD DIVIDED: SUPERPOWER RELATIONS, 1943-72

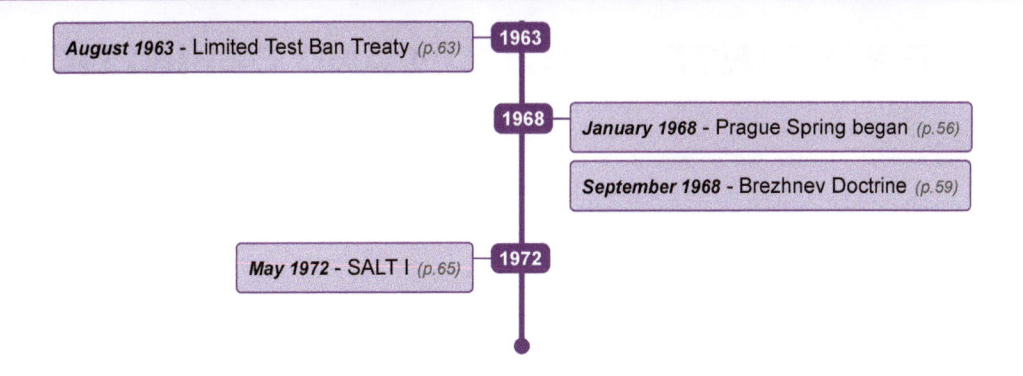

- **1963** — *August 1963* - Limited Test Ban Treaty *(p.63)*
- **1968** — *January 1968* - Prague Spring began *(p.56)*
- **1968** — *September 1968* - Brezhnev Doctrine *(p.59)*
- **1972** — *May 1972* - SALT I *(p.65)*

# COLD WAR INTRODUCTION AND DEFINITION

*'Let us not be deceived - we are today in the midst of a cold war. Our enemies are to be found abroad and at home. Let us never forget this: our unrest is the heart of their success. The peace of the world is the hope and the goal of our political system; it is the despair and defeat of those who stand against us.' - Bernard Baruch 1947*

### What was the Cold War?

The Cold War was a state of hostility that existed between the USSR and the USA in the second half of the 20th century.

### What is the definition of a cold war?

A cold war is a conflict in which there is no direct fighting between the two sides. It is fought through economic and political actions.

### When was the Cold War?

The Cold War lasted from 1945 to 1991.

### Who was involved in the Cold War?

The Cold War was between the USA and its allies, and the Soviet Union, its satellite states and its allies.

### What were the long-term causes of the Cold War?

There are 7 main reasons the Cold War happened:

- In October 1917, the Bolsheviks seized power in Russia. By 1921 they had created the first communist state. They were anti-capitalism and wanted to spread the communist revolution across the world.
- America and Britain did not trust the USSR as Russia had withdrawn from the First World War in 1917, despite being a member of the Triple Entente with Britain and France.
- The USSR did not trust the USA, France and Britain because they sent troops to fight against the Bolsheviks in the Russian Civil War *(p.16)*.
- In the 1920s, the USA suffered from the First Red Scare and was hostile towards the USSR.
- The USSR was angry it was not recognised as a country by the USA until 1933.
- The relationship between the USSR and the West deteriorated before the Second World War. The Soviet Union was angry at not being invited to the Munich Conference in 1938.
- When the USSR signed the Nazi-Soviet Pact in 1939, Britain and France were horrified.

### How was the Cold War fought?

The Cold War was fought in 7 key ways:

- Propaganda.
- Spying or espionage, such as using spy planes to take photographs.
- An arms race to have the most developed weapons, particularly nuclear missiles.
- A space race competing for success in space, such as being the first nation to put a man on the moon.
- Financial aid or loans to other countries to gain their support.
- Proxy wars, where the USA and the USSR became involved in conflicts in other countries. An example is the Korean War *(p.37)* of 1950-53.
- Threats made by either side.

### What created tension between the Soviet Union and the USA at the beginning of the Cold War?

The ideological differences between the superpowers created tension between them. The Soviet Union supported communism, whereas the USA and Britain were capitalist countries.

## What were the different ideologies in the Cold War?
The Cold War was a result of ideological differences between the two sides:
- ☑ The USSR was communist. Communism is a system where there is no private ownership of land, property or business. The aim is to achieve economic equality for the benefit of the people through central control of the state economy.
- ☑ The USA was capitalist. Capitalism is a system where individuals are free to own land, property and businesses to create wealth and accept there will be economic inequality as a result.

## Why were the USA and the USSR considered superpowers during the Cold War?
The USSR and the USA were considered to be superpowers because they possessed 3 key things:
- ☑ Massive military might, including nuclear weapons.
- ☑ Economic might.
- ☑ The ability to dominate other countries.

## Why was Stalin distrustful of Truman at the beginning at the Cold War?
Joseph Stalin was distrustful of Harry S Truman for 3 key reasons:
- ☑ Truman was anti-communist.
- ☑ He tried to control the Potsdam meeting.
- ☑ He successfully tested the atomic bomb *(p.23)* without consulting Stalin and used it in the Hiroshima and Nagasaki bombings in the days after Potsdam.

## Why did Britain ally closely with the USA at the beginning at the Cold War?
Britain was concerned about communism spreading. The nation's economy was severely impacted after the Second World War so it couldn't act against the Soviet Union alone.

### DID YOU KNOW?
**There is a lot of debate about when the Cold War really began, since it was never openly declared.**

Some suggest it started with the American bombing of Hiroshima and Nagasaki, while others claim it goes right back to the Russian Revolution in 1917.

# RUSSIAN REVOLUTION

*'I suddenly realised that the devout Russian people no longer needed priests to pray them into heaven. On earth they were building a kingdom more bright than any heaven had to offer, and for which it was a glory to die' - John Reed, '10 Days that Shook the World'*

## What was the Russian Revolution?
In 1917 the Bolshevik Party overthrew the Russian government and created the world's first communist state. Russia withdrew from the First World War and was plunged into civil war.

## What was the impact of the Russian revolution on the Cold War?
The roots of the Cold War *(p.14)* can be traced back to the Russian Revolution. It led to tension and distrust between the USSR and the USA which was brought to a head with the defeat of Hitler in 1945.

> **DID YOU KNOW?**
>
> **There were two revolutions in Russia in 1917.**
> The one in February abolished the monarchy while the second, in October, brought the Bolsheviks to power on their slogan of 'Peace, Bread and Land'.

# RUSSIAN CIVIL WAR

*'Every person present here knows that perhaps this very evening they will be fighting in front of their own house, that they will perhaps be killed, that if they are taken alive they will be hanged, or shot, or tortured, that the city has only enough bread for twenty four hours, that the greatest powers in the world, the Entente, America, are relentlessly seeking their death and that of all their comrades.' - Victor Serge*

### What was the Russian Civil War?

A civil war was triggered by opposition to the Bolsheviks from various groups, including monarchists who wanted the tsar back in power, anti-communists, groups angered by Brest-Litovsk and different nationalities who wanted their independence.

### When was the Russian Civil War?

The Russian Civil War took place from 1918 to 1921.

### Who fought in the Russian Civil War?

The Russian Civil War was fought between communist (Red) and anti-communist (White) forces. In addition, a number of countries, including Britain and the USA, sent troops to support the Whites. The Reds won.

### What were the different armies involved in the Russian Civil War?

There were 3 main groups involved:
- The Red Army, who were the Bolsheviks or communists.
- The White Army, made up of nationalists and monarchists.
- The Green Army was formed by the peasants.

### What were the causes of the Russian Civil War?

There were 5 key reasons why the Russian Civil War happened:
- The Russian Empire had collapsed because many nationalities wanted independence and the Bolshevik Decree on Nationalities allowed this. People who were pro-Empire wanted to re-conquer these areas.
- Political opposition had grown towards the Bolsheviks from the Social Revolutionaries, the Mensheviks, the Constituent Assembly, and the anti-Bolshevik alliance to form the Whites. People objected to the fact the Bolsheviks had seized power undemocratically.
- The Allies were opposed to the Bolsheviks pulling out of the First World War and the signing of the Treaty of Brest-Litovsk. They hoped that by supporting the Whites, the Bolsheviks would be defeated and Russia would re-enter the war.
- Law and order had broken down.
- Food requisitioning by the Bolsheviks angered the peasants and so they formed the Green Army to defend their homes.

## What were the consequences of the Russian Civil War on international relations?

The Russian Civil War had 3 main consequences for international relations:

- ☑ It increased the Soviet Union's suspicion that the capitalist West would always seek to overthrow communism.
- ☑ In order to protect the USSR from future foreign interference, Lenin, the leader of the USSR, pursued a policy of worldwide communist revolution.
- ☑ This in turn caused a 'Red Scare' in 1920s America as many feared the worldwide spread of communism.

## Who fought against the Bolsheviks in the Russian Civil War?

There were 3 main groups that opposed the Bolsheviks:

- ☑ The Whites consisted of lots of different groups such as Socialist Revolutionaries, tsarists/monarchists, Liberals, ultra-conservatives, and army officers against the Treaty of Brest-Litovsk.
- ☑ The Greens consisted of peasants and deserters from other armies.
- ☑ Foreign countries also intervened in the civil war against the Bolsheviks. Britain, Japan and USA all interfered.

## What were the key events of the Russian Civil war?

There were 9 key events during the Russian Civil War:

- ☑ Trotsky became the Commissar for War for the Bolsheviks and took charge of the Red Army on 13th March, 1918.
- ☑ In May 1918, the Czech Legion rebelled against the Red Army. They were leaving Russia when Trotsky demanded their weapons. They responded by allying with the Socialist Revolutionaries and taking over parts of the Trans-Siberian Railway.
- ☑ On 17th July, 1918, Tsar Nicholas II and his family were executed in Yekaterinburg to prevent the Whites and the Czech Legion from rescuing them and using them as a rallying point in the Civil War.
- ☑ In August 1918, Trotsky increased the harsh discipline in the Red Army so that one in every ten soldiers was shot if he retreated.
- ☑ The Bolsheviks suffered a major set-back during the Eastern Front Offensive led by one of the White's leaders, Admiral Kolchak. He attacked in June 1918. However, the Red Army managed to force the Whites to retreat by June 1919.
- ☑ By October 1919, the Red Army had managed to stop General Yudenich's advance on Petrograd and General Denikin's advance on Moscow.
- ☑ Between April and October 1920, the Bolsheviks were also at war with Poland until they signed the Treaty of Riga in October.
- ☑ The Whites were finally defeated at the Battle of Perekop between 7th and 15th November, 1920.
- ☑ In 1921, the Green Army, led by General Makhno, was finally defeated in the Ukraine and by General Antonov in Tambov where about 50,000 peasants had led an uprising against the Bolsheviks.

## Why did the Bolsheviks win the Russian Civil War?

There are 6 main reasons why the Bolsheviks won:

- ☑ The Bolsheviks had control of the industrial heartlands and transport links, which gave them a great advantage over their enemies. They had control over factories which made munitions.
- ☑ The Bolsheviks had a strong, well-organised propaganda machine and used art, posters and entertainment to spread their message.
- ☑ They introduced conscription into the Red Army so they had five million soldiers by 1921.
- ☑ As commissar for war, Trotsky introduced harsh military discipline, recruited tsarist officers for their experience and used the agitprop trains to spread propaganda. He turned the Red Army into an effective force and his harsh discipline ensured loyalty to the Reds.
- ☑ The Red Terror undermined opposition to the Bolsheviks as the Cheka, or secret police, executed 50,000 of their enemies in 1918 including the tsar and his family.

- Lenin's economic policy of War Communism took control of food production and manufacturing, which ensured the army was supplied.

## Why did the Whites lose the Russian Civil War?

There were 6 key reasons why the Whites lost the civil war:

- They were reliant on foreign assistance for supplies and money, so the Whites were portrayed as the invading army.
- There was a severe lack of planning because they did not have one single leader as it was not a unified group.
- There were problems with communication, geographical distances and rivalry between the leaders.
- They were not united by a single goal as some wanted a return to tsarism, others favoured a military dictatorship and others preferred the Constituent Assembly.
- The Whites did not control the major areas of industry, population or transport links because they tended to be on the outer edges of Russia.
- As a result their army was smaller and not as well supplied.

## What were the consequences of the Russian Civil War?

There were 5 main consequences of the civil war.

- The Bolsheviks consolidated their control over the country, economically with the policy of War Communism and politically as they destroyed their opposition using the Red Terror and by winning the civil war.
- The policy of War Communism left the country economically ruined as food production and manufacturing collapsed.
- There was unrest with strikes and several different peasant uprisings, including the Tambov Uprising from 1920 to 1921, and the Kronstadt Uprising in 1921.
- Around eight million people died.
- The leaders of the Bolshevik Party centralised control over their party as well as the country. All decisions were made by seven to nine key members of the Politburo and orders were passed down to the rank and file.

> **DID YOU KNOW?**
>
> **Their victory in the Russian Civil War centralised the Bolsheviks' control of the country and their own party.**
>
> Power was centralised in the Politburo, the key decision-making body of the Communist Party.

# GRAND ALLIANCE

*'The Russian danger... is our danger' - Winston Churchill*

## What was the Grand Alliance?

The Grand Alliance was a military and political coalition against the Axis powers of Nazi Germany, Italy, and Japan during the Second World War.

## When was the Grand Alliance formed?

The Grand Alliance began after the USA entered the Second World War. The alliance was formally signed by the USA, the Soviet Union and Great Britain on New Year's Day, 1942, and lasted until 1945.

### Who was part of the Grand Alliance?

The Grand Alliance consisted of the three major Allies of the Second World War - the Soviet Union, the United States, and Great Britain.

### Why was the Grand Alliance formed?

The sole purpose of the Grand Alliance was to defeat the Axis powers - Nazi Germany, fascist Italy and Imperial Japan.

### Why was there tension in the Grand Alliance?

Although they were fighting the Nazi threat together, there were 3 main reasons for tension between the countries of the Grand Alliance during the Second World War:

- Both sides kept secrets. Stalin refused to share battle plans with Britain and France; when German troops surrendered in Italy, Britain and the US did not include the USSR in the discussions.
- Stalin believed the USA had deliberately delayed opening a second front in France until 1944 so the USSR would be weakened fighting Nazi Germany on its own.
- The two sides had opposing ideologies and did not trust each other.

### How did the Grand Alliance cooperate during the Second World War?

The public was presented with a positive image of the Grand Alliance, and the three countries did help each other in 3 key ways:

- British merchant ships helped take supplies to the USSR.
- America included the USSR in its Lend-Lease programme, which meant it lent and sold military equipment to help defeat Germany.
- The USSR lost 26 million people fighting the Nazis after 1941, but this meant Germany's army was tied down and allowed Britain and America to plan and launch D-Day.

> **DID YOU KNOW?**
>
> The Grand Alliance is often referred to as a 'marriage of convenience'.
>
> The USSR and the USA put aside their ideological differences to fight a common enemy, Nazi Germany.

## TEHRAN CONFERENCE, 1943

*The Tehran Conference was held to decide how the Second World War would be won.*

### What was the Tehran Conference?

The Tehran Conference was the first of three strategic meetings between the USA, Britain and the Soviet Union to discuss Nazi Germany and how to end the war.

### Who attended the Tehran Conference?

The three Allied leaders who attended the Tehran Conference were:

- President Franklin D Roosevelt of the United States.
- General Secretary Joseph Stalin of the USSR.

- ✓ Prime Minister Winston Churchill *(p.68)* of the United Kingdom.

### Where was the Tehran Conference held?
It was held at the Soviet Union's embassy in Tehran, Iran.

### When was the Tehran Conference held?
The Tehran Conference was held from November to December, 1943.

### Why was the Tehran Conference important?
The Tehran Conference was important for 3 main reasons:
- ✓ It led to a better relationship between the USA, Britain and the USSR.
- ✓ They were working together to defeat Nazi Germany, fascist Italy and Imperial Japan.
- ✓ They also discussed plans for the UN and ending the war.

### What decisions were taken at the Tehran Conference?
There were 5 important decisions made at the Tehran Conference:
- ✓ It was decided the USA and Britain would open a second front by invading Europe through Nazi-occupied France.
- ✓ The USSR would invade Nazi Germany from the east.
- ✓ The USSR would invade Japan once Nazi Germany was defeated.
- ✓ The Polish border would be moved to the west, so Poland would gain territory from Germany and lose it to the USSR from the east.
- ✓ An international organisation would be created to settle international disagreements once the war was over. This would eventually become the United Nations.

### What signs of tension were there at the Tehran Conference?
There were 2 key signs of tension at the Tehran Conference:
- ✓ Churchill *(p.68)* wanted the second front to be opened up in the Balkans, not in France.
- ✓ Roosevelt viewed Britain's colonialism as a greater threat than communism.

---

**DID YOU KNOW?**

Tehran was the first time Roosevelt, Churchill and Stalin all met.

---

# YALTA CONFERENCE, FEB 1945
*The Yalta Conference was held to decide what would happen after the war.*

### What was the Yalta Conference?
The Yalta Conference was the second of three strategic meetings between the USA, Britain and the Soviet Union to discuss winning the war and post-war Europe.

### Where was the Yalta Conference held?
The Yalta Conference took place in Yalta in the USSR.

## When was the Yalta Conference held?

The Yalta Conference was held in February 1945.

## Who attended the Yalta Conference?

The three Allied leaders present at the Yalta Conference were:

- President Roosevelt of the USA.
- General Secretary Stalin of the USSR.
- Prime Minister Churchill *(p.68)* of Great Britain.

## What decisions were taken at the Yalta Conference?

There were 11 important decisions made at the Yalta Conference.

- The superpowers agreed on the Declaration of Liberated Europe which guaranteed all countries freed from Nazi control the right to hold democratic and free elections.
- Nazi Germany and Berlin would be divided into four zones controlled by the USA, Britain, France and the Soviet Union.
- Germany would be reduced in size.
- Germany would be demilitarised.
- Germany would be ordered to pay reparations.
- Nazi war criminals would be tried after the war was over and the Nazi Party banned.
- Poland would fall under the Soviet sphere of influence.
- Poland would be run under a democratically elected government.
- Eastern Europe would have free elections.
- The USSR would declare war on Japan 3 months after Nazi Germany was defeated.
- The United Nations was created.

## What disagreements were there at the Yalta Conference?

There were 3 main disagreements at the Yalta Conference:

- The USSR wanted Germany to pay high reparations; Britain and the USA disagreed.
- Britain and the USA wanted Germany to recover, whereas the USSR wanted to keep Germany weak.
- Stalin wanted the Polish-German border to be much further to the west and desired a 'friendly' Polish government. Britain and the USA were worried this would mean Poland would be controlled by the USSR.

---

### DID YOU KNOW?

**The Yalta Conference was the final one attended by Stalin, Roosevelt and Churchill.**

President Roosevelt died before the Potsdam Conference and Churchill lost the general election in Great Britain to the Labour Party in July 1945.

# POTSDAM CONFERENCE, JULY 1945

*The Potsdam Conference came a few months after Yalta. There was significant tension between the USSR and the USA over the issue of the atomic bomb.*

### What was the Potsdam Conference?

The Potsdam Conference was the third and final meeting between the USA, Britain and the Soviet Union to discuss Nazi Germany and the future of Europe.

### Where was the Potsdam Conference held?

The Potsdam Conference was held in Potsdam, Germany.

### When was the Potsdam Conference held?

The Potsdam Conference took place between July and August 1945.

### Who attended the Potsdam Conference?

The three Allied leaders who met at Potsdam were:

- President Harry Truman *(p.74)* of the United States.
- Prime Minister Clement Attlee of Great Britain.
- Premier Joseph Stalin of the Soviet Union.

### Why did the leaders at the Potsdam Conference change?

Leadership of two Allied nations had changed since the Yalta Conference *(p.20)*. Roosevelt died in April 1945 and Churchill *(p.68)* lost the British general election in July.

### What disagreements were there at the Potsdam Conference?

There were 4 key areas of disagreement:

- The USA and Britain were unhappy Stalin had removed the non-communists from the Polish Provisional Government of National Unity.
- The USA and Britain were unhappy Stalin had not allowed free elections in eastern Europe. Stalin was angry as he thought the West was interfering.
- Truman deliberately delayed the Potsdam meeting so America could test the atomic bomb *(p.23)*. When Truman informed Stalin about the USA's successful test, Stalin was very angry not to have been told beforehand.
- Truman was very anti-communist and wanted to get 'tough' with Stalin.

### What decisions were taken at the Potsdam Conference?

There were 8 important decisions made at the Potsdam Conference:

- The Nazi Party was banned.
- War criminals were to be prosecuted.
- Germany was to be reduced in size.
- Germany would be divided into four occupied zones controlled by the USA, Britain, France and the Soviet Union.
- Berlin would also be divided into four occupied zones controlled by the USA, Britain, France and the Soviet Union.
- All economic decisions about Germany must be agreed to by all four powers in the Allied Control Council.
- A Council of Foreign Ministers was set up to organise the rebuilding of Europe.
- It was decided the Soviet Union would receive 25% of the industrial output from the other three occupied zones.

> **DID YOU KNOW?**
>
> Roosevelt's death of a haemorrhagic stroke in 1945 before the Potsdam Conference was unexpected. America and the world were shocked.
>
> Half a million people attended his funeral procession.

# THE ATOMIC BOMB

*'I am become death, the destroyer of worlds.' - Oppenheimer, a key scientist in the creation of the nuclear bomb, on witnessing a test detonation*

### How did the atomic bomb affect the Cold War?

America's use of nuclear weapons against Japan in 1945 increased tension and distrust between the superpowers.

### Why did America use nuclear weapons?

There is disagreement about why America did this. There are 2 main theories.

- The first theory says the Americans had no choice. Japan had been allied with Nazi Germany during the Second World War, and the USA believed the use of nuclear weapons would force the Japanese to surrender.
- The second theory is that the Americans did this as a way of showcasing their military power, to try to intimidate the Soviet Union before the coming Cold War *(p.14)*.

### Who ordered the nuclear bomb to be dropped in 1945?

President Harry Truman *(p.74)* authorised the use of nuclear weapons against Japan.

### Which cities did the Americans attack with nuclear weapons?

The Americans launched nuclear attacks against the Japanese cities of Hiroshima and Nagasaki.

### How many people died when the Americans used nuclear weapons against Japan?

Around 70,000 died in the initial blast at Hiroshima, and a further 40,000 at Nagasaki. Many more died over the coming weeks, months and years from severe burns and radiation poisoning.

### How did the atomic bomb cause tension in the Cold War?

There were 3 key ways that dropping the nuclear bomb affected the Cold War *(p.14)*.

- Truman had deliberately delayed the Potsdam meeting so that America could test the atomic bomb.
- Truman kept the existence of America's nuclear technology a secret until the attack and refused to share the technology. This created distrust and tension with the USSR.
- The dropping of the bomb made the USSR determined to possess its own nuclear weapon to even the stakes. This laid the ground for the later arms race between the superpowers.

> **DID YOU KNOW?**
>
> The USA is the only power to have ever deliberately used nuclear weapons against human targets.

## THE LONG TELEGRAM, 1946

*'It is clear that the main element of any United States policy towards the Soviet Union must be that of a long term, patient, but firm and vigilant containment of Russian expansive tendencies.' - George F Kennan*

### What was the 'Long Telegram'?
The Long Telegram was a secret report sent by the US Ambassador in the Soviet Union, George Kennan, to President Truman.

### When was the 'Long Telegram' sent?
The 'Long Telegram' was sent on 22nd February, 1946.

### Who sent the 'Long Telegram'?
George Kennan, the US Ambassador in the Soviet Union, sent the 'Long Telegram'.

### Where was the 'Long Telegram' sent?
The 'Long Telegram' was sent to Washington from the United States Embassy in Moscow.

### What did the 'Long Telegram' say?
The 'Long Telegram' stated:
- The USSR was a threat to capitalism and should be eliminated.
- The USSR was building its military power.
- Peace between the USA and the USSR was not possible.
- The USSR was determined to expand.

> **DID YOU KNOW?**
>
> **The 'Long Telegram' acquired its name because it was much longer than a normal telegram.**
>
> It contained more than 5,000 words, whereas telegrams were usually very brief. This showed the urgency of Kennan's message.

# THE NOVIKOV TELEGRAM, 1946

*The Novikov Telegram was very influenctial on the USSR's behaviour in eastern Europe.*

### What was the Novikov Telegram?
The Novikov Telegram was a secret report sent to Stalin.

### When was the Novikov Telegram sent?
It was sent in September 1946.

### Who sent the Novikov Telegram?
Nikolai Novikov, the Soviet Ambassador in the USA, sent the Novikov Telegram.

### Where was the Novikov Telegram sent?
The Novikov Telegram was sent from the Soviet Embassy in Washington to Moscow.

### What did the Novikov Telegram contain?
The Novikov Telegram stated that:
- ☑ The USA wanted to be the world's leading power.
- ☑ The USSR was the only power that could stand up to them.
- ☑ The USA was preparing for war against the Soviets.

> **DID YOU KNOW?**
>
> Novikov wrote in his telegram: 'All of these facts show clearly that a decisive role in the realization of plans for world dominance by the United States is played by its armed forces.'

# SATELLITE STATES, 1946-49

*After the Second World War, Stalin insisted on a protective 'buffer' of satellite states for the USSR.*

### What were the Soviet satellite states?
The Soviet satellite states were countries in eastern Europe under the political, economic and military influence of the USSR.

### Who were the Soviet satellite states?
They were Poland, Czechoslovakia, Hungary, Romania, Bulgaria and East Germany.

### When were the Soviet satellite states created?
The satellite states were created between 1946 and 1949.

### What methods were used to create the Soviet satellite states?
There are 2 key things to note about the methods used:

- In the late 1940s, Stalin installed communist leaders in eastern European countries using 'salami tactics'.
- The term 'salami tactics' was coined by the communist Hungarian leader, Matyas Rakosi, to describe how Stalin dealt with opposition 'slice by slice'.

### How were the Soviet satellite states created?

There were 5 main ways in which the Soviet Union took over eastern European countries:

- The Red Army supported communists and intimidated the opposition. They acted as an occupying force.
- Elections were held and as a result the communists were part of coalition governments.
- The communists worked in coalitions to undermine the government and held key positions, such as head of the police, so they could arrest and murder opponents.
- Propaganda was used to label any opposition party or leader a fascist to boost support for communist parties or to demonise democratic politicians.
- Once in government, communist parties, aided by the security forces, rigged elections to ensure they remained in power.

### What was the importance of the Soviet satellite states?

The satellite states helped the Soviet Union in 4 key ways:

- It meant the USSR had gained a large territory with which it could trade.
- They enhanced its power.
- In theory, they strengthened communism.
- They acted as a buffer zone to protect the USSR from invasion.

### What were the different points of view about the Soviet satellite states?

There are 2 key things to note about how satellite states are viewed:

- Stalin viewed the satellite states as a necessary buffer against future invasion from Germany in particular.
- However, Britain and the USA saw them as a threat to the West.

> **DID YOU KNOW?**
>
> The countries of eastern Europe were called satellite states in the West because they were effectively controlled by the USSR and positioned closely around its border, like satellites clustered around a planet.

# IRON CURTAIN SPEECH, 1946

*'From Stettin in the Baltic, to Trieste in the Adriatic, an iron curtain has descended across the continent.' - Winston Churchill, 1947*

### What was the 'Iron Curtain' speech?

Winston Churchill *(p.68)*, although no longer the prime minister of Britain, gave a significant speech where he described how Europe had been divided by an 'iron curtain'. This analogy described the USSR's actions in eastern Europe that had divided Europe in two.

### When was the 'Iron Curtain' speech delivered?

Winston Churchill *(p.68)* gave the speech in March 1946.

### Who delivered the 'Iron Curtain' speech?
Winston Churchill *(p.68)* gave the 'Iron Curtain' speech.

### Where was the 'Iron Curtain' speech delivered?
Winston Churchill *(p.68)* gave the speech in Fulton, USA.

### What important argument was made by Churchill during the 'Iron Curtain' speech?
Churchill *(p.68)* argued that:
- Strong American-British relations were essential to stop the spread of communism and maintain peace.
- The USA must play an active role in world affairs.

### Why was the 'Iron Curtain' speech important?
It helped bolster American and western European opposition to communism and the Soviet Union. It worsened relations between the USSR and the West.

### How did Stalin respond to the 'Iron Curtain' speech?
Stalin responded to the 'Iron Curtain' speech by:
- Comparing Churchill *(p.68)* to Hitler and claiming Churchill was attempting to draw racial boundaries.
- Calling Churchill *(p.68)* a warmonger (someone who encourages or seeks war).

> **DID YOU KNOW?**
> Some regard Churchill's 'Iron Curtain' speech as the real beginning of the Cold War, because it was one of the first public announcements of hostility.

## TRUMAN DOCTRINE, 1947
*'The seeds of totalitarian regimes are nurtured by misery and want. They spread and grow in the evil soil of poverty and strife.' - Harry Truman*

### What was the Truman Doctrine?
The Truman Doctrine was an American policy which was anti-communist and involved the containment of communism. It led to the Marshall Plan *(p.28)*.

### When did the Truman Doctrine begin?
President Harry S Truman announced his doctrine on 12th March, 1947.

### Why was the Truman Doctrine established?
There were 3 main reasons the Truman Doctrine was created:
- Britain could not afford to give any more military support to the Greek government in the civil war against Greek communists.
- The USA promised $400 million in aid to Greece and Turkey to help win the war against the Greek communists.

- It aimed to contain the spread of communism by giving military and economic assistance to any country threatened by communism.

### What were the main points of the Truman Doctrine?

The Truman Doctrine contained 3 key points:
- It stated the world had a choice between communism, or capitalism and democracy;
- The USA would send troops and economic aid to countries threatened by communism so it was contained and could not spread;
- The USA would no longer follow an isolationist foreign policy and would now get involved in the affairs of other countries, rather than stay out of them.

### What conditions were there in order for countries to receive aid under the Truman Doctrine?

Countries had to choose capitalism over communism in order to receive aid from the USA.

### What was the importance of the Truman Doctrine?

There were 4 main reasons the Truman Doctrine was important:
- It meant the USA officially abandoned its isolationist foreign policy and would play an active role in the world.
- It meant the USA was on a potential collision course with the USSR as the doctrine was directed against the spread of communism.
- It directly resulted in the creation of the Marshall Plan *(p.28)*.
- It resulted in the further deterioration in the relationship between the USA and the USSR.

> **DID YOU KNOW?**
> The Truman Doctrine was the first American policy that expressed the need to contain the spread of communism.

# MARSHALL PLAN, 1947

*'Our policy is directed not against any country or doctrine, but against hunger, poverty, desperation and chaos.' - Harry Truman*

### What was the Marshall Plan?

The Marshall Plan was a scheme to provide economic aid to Europe.

### When was the Marshall Plan introduced?

The Marshall Plan was introduced in 1948.

### Who came up with the Marshall Plan?

It was proposed by the US Secretary of State, George C Marshall.

### Why was the Marshall Plan introduced?

The Marshall Plan was essentially the Truman Doctrine *(p.27)* in action. By making countries dependent on US dollars, it would prevent the spread of communism.

### How much money was provided by the Marshall Plan?
$13.3 billion was provided by the USA to help rebuild Europe.

### Which countries received aid under the Marshall Plan?
A total of 16 western European countries, including France, West Germany and Britain, received aid.

### What was it hoped would be achieved by the Marshall Plan?
It was feared the damage and poverty caused by the Second World War would encourage people to turn to communism. Giving countries money to rebuild would stop them becoming communist.

### What were the conditions needed to receive aid from the Marshall Plan?
In order to receive money, countries had to trade with the USA and be capitalist.

### What was the reaction to the Marshall Plan?
The USSR reacted in 4 main ways to the Marshall Plan:
- The Soviet Union saw both the Truman Doctrine *(p.27)* and the Marshall Plan as a threat to communism.
- Stalin called it 'dollar imperialism' and claimed the USA was trying to take over Europe using its economic strength.
- Stalin responded by creating Cominform *(p.29)* in 1947, which coordinated and controlled communist parties in Europe from the USSR.
- Comecon *(p.30)* was established in 1949 to organise economic trade between eastern Europe and the USSR.

### What was the significance of the Marshall Plan?
The Marshall Plan was significant for 4 key reasons:
- It helped the economic recovery of western Europe.
- It limited the expansion of Soviet influence in Europe so the USSR was 'contained'.
- It deepened the divide between western Europe and eastern Europe as they were now divided politically and economically.
- It worsened the relationship between the USA and the USSR.

---

**DID YOU KNOW?**

If the USA spent the same proportion of its GDP on aid today as during the Marshall Plan, it would amount to $800 billion dollars.

---

## COMINFORM, 1947

*The Cominform described the world as divided into two sharply drawn camps: the camp of imperialism and war, headed by the United States, and the camp of socialism and peace, headed by the Soviet Union.*

### What was Cominform?
Cominform was the Communist Information Bureau. It organised all communist parties in Europe under the USSR's control.

### When was Cominform created?
The Communist Information Bureau was created in September 1947.

### Who were the members of Cominform?
Members included the USSR, France, Italy, Czechoslovakia, Bulgaria, Poland, Yugoslavia and Romania.

### Why was Cominform created?
Cominform was created for 2 key reasons:
- It was a reaction to the creation of the Marshall Plan *(p.28)* by the USA.
- It was a way in which the USSR could control all communist parties in Europe.

### Why was Cominform important?
Cominform meant that the USSR politically controlled all communist parties in eastern Europe. It created a trade network between communist countries.

> **DID YOU KNOW?**
> The leader of Yugoslavia, General Tito, resisted being controlled by Cominform.
> As a result, he was expelled from the bureau in 1948.

## COMECON, 1949
*Comecon was seen as the Soviet 'answer' to the Marshall Plan.*

### What was Comecon?
Comecon was the Council for Mutual Economic Assistance. It was the Soviet Union's alternative to the Marshall Plan *(p.28)*.

### When was Comecon created?
Comecon was created in January 1949.

### Who was part of Comecon?
Comecon included the Soviet Union, Bulgaria, Czechoslovakia, Poland, Romania, Hungary, Albania and the German Democratic Republic (East Germany).

### Why was Comecon created?
Comecon was a reaction to the Marshall Plan *(p.28)*, introduced by the USA, and was created for 2 main reasons:
- Stalin wanted to reduce any possible economic influence the USA could have on eastern Europe's communist countries by creating his own version of the Marshall Plan *(p.28)*.
- It was a method of controlling the satellite states in eastern Europe by tying them into close trading relationships with the USSR and each other.

## What was the importance of Comecon?

Comecon, with the Marshall Plan *(p.28)*, divided Europe into two economic spheres of influence; western European was capitalist and eastern European was communist.

> **DID YOU KNOW?**
> Comecon was used to develop closer ties between the USSR and the countries of eastern Europe.

# BERLIN BLOCKADE, 1948-49

*The Berlin Blockade was seen as an aggressive move by Stalin, designed to establish dominance over Berlin and Germany.*

## What was the Berlin Blockade?

The USSR closed all road, rail and river transport links into West Berlin. This stopped all supplies getting into the city. British, French and US troops were asked to leave.

## When was the Berlin Blockade?

The Berlin Blockade started in June 1948 and ended in May 1949.

## What caused the Berlin Blockade?

There were 8 key causes of the Berlin Blockade:

- The growing tension between the USA and the USSR over the future of Germany.
- The growing tension between the USA and the USSR because of their ideological differences and the start of the Cold War *(p.14)*.
- In January 1947, the British and USA joined their zones, creating 'Bizonia'. This broke the agreements made at the Potsdam Conference *(p.22)*.
- In December 1947, at the London Conference, Britain, France and the USA met to discuss Germany and decide Germany's new constitution. The USSR was not included.
- In March 1948, France's zone joined Bizonia to create 'Trizonia'.
- The USSR left the Allied Control Commission, accusing the West of breaking the Potsdam agreements. They were angry the London Conference had taken place.
- In April 1948, Trizonia started to receive Marshall Aid *(p.28)* and began to rebuild.
- Britain, France and the USA introduced a new 'safe' currency, the Deutschmark, into Trizonia on 23rd June, 1948, which angered the USSR.

## What were the consequences of the Berlin Blockade?

There were 3 main consequences of the Berlin Blockade:

- It prevented supplies reaching West Berlin.
- It led to the Berlin Airlift *(p.32)* from June 1948 to May 1949, in which the Western powers used airplanes to fly supplies into West Berlin.
- The relationship between the USSR and the West deteriorated further, eventually leading to the creation of NATO *(p.34)*.

*Get our free app at GCSEHistory.com*

**What was the significance of the Berlin Blockade?**

The Berlin Blockade was significant for 2 key reasons:

- The West saw it as an act of aggression by Stalin.
- It created the first major crisis between the USA and the USSR in the Cold War *(p.14)*.

> **DID YOU KNOW?**
>
> The blockade lasted 318 days (11 months).

# BERLIN AIRLIFT, 1948-49

*Rather than risk war over the Blockade, the Americans circumnavigated it with the Berlin Airlift.*

**What did the western powers do in response to the Berlin Blockade?**

Western powers responded to the blockade of West Berlin by organising an airlift. Supplies were flown into West Berlin every day.

**When was the Berlin Airlift?**

The Berlin Airlift saw supplies flown into Berlin every day from 26th June, 1948, to 12th May, 1949.

**Why did the Berlin Airlift happen?**

There were 3 main reasons the Berlin Airlift occurred:

- The West did not want to be forced out of West Berlin because Stalin would be able to take over.
- The USA wanted to contain communism, as promised in the Truman Doctrine *(p.27)*.
- It was a way to get around the blockade without starting a war.

**What happened during the Berlin Airlift?**

There were 3 key events during the Berlin Airlift:

- Britain, France and the USA flew in supplies of food, medicine and fuel throughout the Blockade.
- By the end of the Blockade, approximately 8,000 tonnes of supplies were being flown in every day.
- A new airport called Berlin-Tegel was built and a new runway was built at Berlin-Tempelhof to cope with the number of planes flying in supplies.

**What were the consequences of the Berlin Airlift?**

There were 4 key consequences of the Berlin Airlift:

- Two Germanies were created; The Federal Republic of Germany (West Germany) in May 1949 and the German Democratic Republic (East Germany) in October 1949.
- It led to the USA creating a military alliance called NATO *(p.34)* in April 1949.
- Europe was divided even more: politically (capitalism versus communism), economically (Marshall Aid *(p.28)* versus Comecon *(p.30)*), and now militarily.
- The balance of power became more unstable when the USSR conducted its first successful atomic bomb *(p.23)* test in August 1949.

> **DID YOU KNOW?**
>
> The Americans carried a total of 2,245,315 tons of supplies into Berlin during the airlift.

# TWO GERMANIES

*The creation of two German nations was not the Grand Alliance's intention when it split Germany into 4 zones during the wartime meetings.*

### What was the division of Germany?
Germany was split into two countries, the Federal Republic of Germany and the German Democratic Republic.

### When was the division of Germany?
Germany was first split into two countries when, in May 1949, the Federal Republic of Germany - popularly known as West Germany - was created. The German Democratic Republic - or East Germany - was formed in October 1949.

### Why did the division of Germany happen?
Germany was divided into two countries for 2 key reasons:
- The decisions made at the Yalta and Potsdam Conferences resulted in Germany being split into 4 zones under the control of the USSR, France, Britain and the USA.
- The increasing tension between the Western powers (Britain, France and the USA) and the East (the USSR) over the future of Germany.

### How did the division of Germany happen?
There were 6 key events that led to the division of Germany:
- This increased tension resulted in the Berlin Crisis *(p.49)* when Stalin blockaded Berlin to force the Western powers out of West Berlin.
- The West responded with the Berlin Airlift *(p.32)*.
- Three days after Stalin called off the blockade, the West decided to formally unite their 3 zones into the Federal Republic of Germany on 8th May, 1949.
- The new parliament, the Bundestag, of the Federal Republic of Germany was founded in Bonn on 14th August, 1949.
- After elections, Konrad Adenauer was appointed the first chancellor of the Federal Republic of Germany on 15th September, 1949.
- The USSR responded by formally turning the eastern zone into the German Democratic Republic in October 1949.

### Where were the capital cities after the division of Germany?
There were now 2 capital cities, one in each of the divided Germanies:
- The capital of the Federal Republic of Germany was moved to the city of Bonn.
- The capital of the German Democratic Republic was the eastern sector of Berlin controlled by the USSR after the Second World War.

### What was the relationship like between the two Germanies after the division of Germany?

The relationship between the two Germanies was tense for 3 key reasons:

- Each German state recognised only itself as the legitimate German nation.
- The Federal Republic of Germany (West Germany) refused to acknowledge Germany had been divided into two separate countries.
- The German Federal Republic was only recognised as a nation by Eastern Bloc countries and the USSR, not by the Western powers.

> **DID YOU KNOW?**
> The creation of two German nations was an iconic symbol of the divisions of the Cold War.

# NATO, 1949

*'The North Atlantic Treaty Organisation is first and foremost an effective defence alliance. It prevents potential opponents from being tempted to exert political pressure on any one of the allies through military force.' - Willy Brandt, 1968*

### What is NATO?

NATO is an acronym for North Atlantic Treaty Organisation. It is a military alliance based on the promise of mutual defence against an attack by an external force.

### When was NATO formed?

NATO was formed on 4th April, 1949.

### Who joined NATO?

The original 12 members were: the USA, Canada, Great Britain, Belgium, France, Italy, the Netherlands, Norway, Denmark, Luxembourg, Portugal and Iceland.

### Why was NATO created?

NATO was formed by the USA and other western countries for 2 main reasons:

- Stalin and USSR's actions in the Berlin Blockade *(p.31)* had worried them.
- They wanted military protection from future aggression.

### What were the consequences of the creation of NATO?

There were 4 key consequences of the creation of NATO:

- The USSR was contained in Europe, ensuring if it attacked any European member of NATO the other members would help the country under attack.
- All NATO members were protected by the promise of mutual military aid against any Soviet attack, helping to make the security of western Europe stronger.
- In response to West Germany joining NATO, the Soviet Union formed the Warsaw Pact *(p.35)* in 1955 so the USSR had full military control over eastern Europe.
- The USA had committed to a military presence in Europe.

### What message was sent by the creation of NATO?

The creation of NATO sent 2 main messages to the USSR:

- ☑ The USA and western European countries would not accept Soviet aggression.
- ☑ The West would maintain the idea of containment set out in the Truman Doctrine *(p.27)*.

### Why was NATO important?

NATO was important for 2 main reasons:

- ☑ It was based on the idea of 'collective security' - when one country is attacked, the rest must assist it.
- ☑ It acted as a deterrent *(p.60)* to a military attack by the Soviet Union on western Europe.

**DID YOU KNOW?**
NATO still exists today.

## WARSAW PACT, 1955

*The Warsaw Pact was the USSR's answer to the North Atlantic Treaty Organisation - the Soviets hurried to form it after West Germany joined NATO.*

### What was the Warsaw Pact?

The Warsaw Pact was a defensive military alliance between the USSR and eastern European countries.

### When was the Warsaw Pact signed?

The Warsaw Pact was established on 14th May, 1955.

### Who was part of the Warsaw Pact?

The members of the Warsaw Pact were the USSR, Albania, Bulgaria, Czechoslovakia, East Germany, Hungary, Poland and Romania.

### Why was the Warsaw Pact created?

There were 2 key reasons the Warsaw Pact was created:

- ☑ The USSR felt threatened when West Germany was allowed to join NATO *(p.34)* in 1955 because Germany had invaded Russia in both world wars.
- ☑ The Pact would increase the USSR's control over eastern Europe.

### What did the members of the Warsaw Pact agree to?

By joining the Warsaw Pact, members agreed to defend each other if they were attacked by a non-member. This was the idea of collective security.

### What were the consequences of the creation of the Warsaw Pact?

There were 3 main consequences of the creation of the Warsaw Pact:

- ☑ The USSR increased control over the satellite states in eastern Europe because it dominated the Pact.

*Get our free app at GCSEHistory.com*

- Europe was now divided politically, economically and militarily into two hostile camps.
- It intensified the arms race with the West.

> **DID YOU KNOW?**
>
> The USSR heavily prioritised the Warsaw Pact - during the Hungarian Uprising of 1956, it was the Hungarian government's attempt to leave it that provoked the Soviets to invade.

# ARMS RACE

*'I think the bomb instead constitutes merely a first step in a new control by man over the forces of nature too revolutionary and dangerous to fit into old concepts.' - Henry Stimson*

### What was the arms race?
The arms race was a competition between the USA and the USSR to gain military dominance by developing their nuclear capabilities and weapons.

### When was the arms race?
The Soviet Union emerged as a nuclear power in 1949, leading to the arms race with the USA. This lasted until the end of the Cold War *(p.14)* in 1990.

### What was the importance of the arms race?
The arms race was important for 2 main reasons:
- It led to the fear of mutually assured destruction as both sides had enough weapons to destroy the world many times over.
- The USA and the USSR had to find ways to solve disputes that did not result in a nuclear war.

### What were the most important events of the arms race?
There were 6 main military achievements and events during the arms race:
- 1945 - the USA dropped atomic bombs on Hiroshima and Nagasaki, bringing the Second World War to an end.
- 1949 - the USSR tested an atomic bomb *(p.23)*.
- 1952 - the USA developed the hydrogen bomb.
- 1953 - the USSR tested its own hydrogen bomb.
- 1957 - both the USA and USSR successfully tested intercontinental ballistic missiles (ICBMs).
- 1962 - the Cuban Missile Crisis *(p.54)* was the highest point of tension in the arms race.

### What role did brinkmanship play in the arms race?
Brinkmanship was important in the arms race because:
- An enemy could be forced to back down in a moment of crisis by pushing it to the brink of an unwanted war.
- To make any threats credible, both sides needed nuclear weapons.
- The Cuban Missile Crisis *(p.54)* is an example of brinkmanship. The USA and the USSR were very close to a nuclear war, with both sides threatening conflict until the USSR backed down.

### What was the theory of mutually assured destruction, or MAD in the arms race?

Mutually assured destruction, or MAD, was the following theory:

- ✅ It had developed by the 1960s.
- ✅ It stated that if either the USA or the USSR used their nuclear weapons, both would be destroyed. Each possessed so many, the damage would be unimaginable.
- ✅ It was believed war would be prevented because both sides feared it; a nuclear war was, in theory, unwinnable.

### What was nuclear utilisation target selection in the arms race?

Nuclear utilisation target selection theory, or NUTs:

- ✅ Developed in the 1980s.
- ✅ Was a theory President Reagan believed in. He thought a limited nuclear war was possible as long as the USA struck at the USSR first and wiped out its nuclear weapons.

### What were intercontinental ballistic missiles in the arms race?

Intercontinental ballistic missiles, called ICBMs, were nuclear-armed ballistic missiles with a range of more than 3,500 miles.

### What were anti-ballistic missiles in the arms race?

Anti-ballistic missiles were missiles that would intercept and destroy other ballistic missiles. The USA and the USSR developed ABMs in the 1960s.

### What were multiple independent reentry vehicles in the arms race?

Multiple independent reentry vehicles (MIRVs) were developed in 1968. These missiles carried multiple warheads which could each be independently targeted.

---

**DID YOU KNOW?**

In October 1961, the USSR tested its largest nuclear weapon, the Tsar Bomba, creating the most powerful man-made explosion ever seen.

The explosion yielded 58 megatons of TNT and blast waves were recorded as travelling three times around the earth.

---

## THE KOREAN WAR

*America was incredibly concerned when the Korean War began as it appeared to confirm that communism was spreading.*

### What was the Korean War?

The Korean War was fought between North and South Korea and was the first flashpoint of the Cold War in Asia.

### Where did the Korean War take place?

In Korea, which is between China to the west and Japan to the east.

## When was the Korean War?

The Korean War began in June 1950 and finished in 1954.

## What were the key phases of the Korean War?

There were 5 main phases to the war, including:

- North Korea invaded South Korea on 25th June, 1950.
- A UN army, made up mostly of American military and led by General Douglas MacArthur, arrived in Korea in September 1950 to push back against the North Korean invasion *(p.41)*.
- In October 1950, UN forces advanced into North Korean territory.
- On 25th October, China entered the war. Together with the North Korean army, they pushed the UN forces back below the 38th parallel. This resulted in a stalemate for over two years.
- After peace talks on 27th July, 1953, the UN, China and North Korea signed a peace treaty.

## At the end of the Second World War, what was the situation that led to the Korean War?

At the end of the Second World War, when Japan surrendered and Korea was occupied by Soviet troops in the north and American troops in the south, the following happened:

- The country was divided into two separate zones along the 38th parallel, a circle of latitude that runs across the middle of Korea.
- The division of Korea was supposed to be temporary. The aim was for it to be a united and independent country. The United Nations was to organise elections that would achieve this.
- Instead of free elections, the Soviets in North Korea enabled Korean communist Kim Il-Sung to take control of the nation without being elected.
- There was an election in US-controlled South Korea, and USA supporter and capitalist figure Syngman Rhee became its leader.
- At this point, North and South Korea became two different nations. The USSR zone in the north became the People's Republic of Korea, and the US zone in the south became the Republic of Korea.
- While the leaders in both North and South Korea were nationalists and wanted a united country after the war, they wanted the nation to be led by different ideologies - capitalism in the south and communism in the north.

## What were the key events in the build-up to the Korean War?

The leaders of North and South Korea each saw themselves as the legitimate and rightful ruler of the whole nation. Events in the build-up to the Korean War included:

- Due to the attitude of superiority from both sides there were a number of clashes on the border between North and South Korea.
- Kim Il-Sung, the leader of North Korea, visited Stalin in 1949 to ask for his support in an invasion of South Korea. He felt this would be welcome in the south as an effort to reunite the two nations.
- Stalin did not think it was the right time as he did not want a fight against US troops still stationed in South Korea.
- In 1950, Stalin's circumstances had changed. The US troops had left South Korea; communists were in power in China; and the USSR had its own nuclear weapons and had cracked the secret codes used by the USA to talk to other nations. As a result, Stalin felt any future actions in Korea would not meet American opposition.
- Stalin began sending tanks, artillery and aircraft to North Korea and gave the go-ahead for an invasion of the south.
- Stalin stated USSR soldiers would not be directly involved, and if further supplies were needed North Korea should ask China.

## What started the Korean War?

The Korean War broke out when North Korea invaded South Korea on 25th June, 1950.

*Quizzes, amazing exam preparation tools and more at GCSEHistory.com*

### Why did the UN get involved in the Korean War?

When the south was invaded, the USA brought the matter to the UN which passed a resolution calling for North Korea to withdraw. When it did not, the UN sent international troops - mostly American - to force it out. In this way the USA could argue it was acting against international aggression rather than following its containment policy.

### Why did America get involved in the Korean War?

There were 3 key reasons America got involved in the Korean War:

- President Truman was concerned communism was spreading in Asia.
- China's fall to communism in 1949 heightened this fear.
- Truman was also concerned about Stalin's use of Cominform *(p.29)* to encourage countries to turn to communism.

### What was America's role in the Korean War?

America had 2 main roles in the Korean War:

- United Nations troops, mainly American and led by US General Douglas MacArthur, were sent to Korea. The North was supported by the Soviet Union.
- UN forces were able to push North Korea back to the Chinese border, but in late 1950 China joined the war and the UN had to retreat.

### What ended the Korean War?

After three years of fighting an armistice was agreed, which re-established the border between North and South Korea.

### What effect did the Korean War have on America?

There were 5 main consequences of the Korean War:

- It demonstrated the USA's commitment to containing communism and led to a tripling of military spending to prevent its spread.
- To stop the spread of communism in Asia, the Southeast Asia Treaty Organisation (SEATO) was set up in September 1954. Britain, Pakistan, USA, Thailand, France, Australia, the Philippines and New Zealand all joined.
- The sacking of General MacArthur over his proposal to deploy nuclear bombs against North Korea underlined the USA's caution with regard to using nuclear weapons.
- The Soviet Union doubled the size of the Red Army, from 2.8 million in 1950 to 5.6 million in 1955.
- As the war did not escalate further, it showed neither superpower was prepared to engage in direct military confrontation with the other, preferring instead to fight proxy wars.

### What happened in the Korean War?

The fighting in Korea took place in mountains, ravines and swamps - terrain that was more familiar to the Koreans and Chinese than the UN. They also had to contend with terrible cold and snowstorms in winter.

### What were the main events of the Korean War?

The Korean War progressed in a number of stages:

- Between September and October 1950, the UN was successful in pushing North Korean troops back out of South Korea.
- Between October and November 1950, the UN troops crossed over the 38th parallel and pushed the North Korean troops north in an attempt to defeat the communists and reunite the country.
- Between November 1950 and January 1951, Chinese forces launched a counteroffensive and pushed the UN troops back past the 38th parallel.
- The UN counter-attacked between January and July 1951 and retook Seoul.
- The war then settled into a stalemate which lasted for two years, from July 1951 to July 1953.

### How successful was the UN in Korean War?

In the initial stages of their involvement, UN troops were successful in pushing back the North Korean troops.

- Some UN troops joined the South Korean forces in Pusan and pushed past the Pusan perimeter.
- Others, led by General MacArthur, invaded behind the communist lines at Inchon.
- Seoul was liberated from the communists and North Korean troops were pushed back to the 38th parallel.

### Why did the UN invade North Korea during the Korean War?

From October 1950, after UN troops had liberated South Korea, they began to invade North Korea.

- The UN troops crossed the 38th parallel in an attempt to achieve the UN objective of a 'unified, independent and democratic government' for all of Korea.
- Pyongyang was captured on 19th October.
- By November, some American forces had reached the Yalu River on the border with China.

### How did China get involved in the Korean War?

There were 4 key events:

- As UN troops approached its borders, China feared an invasion of its territory and launched a huge counter-attack of 200,000 soldiers.
- UN forces were driven south, back over the 38th parallel.
- Seoul was recaptured by communist forces.
- The UN forces eventually stabilised around the 37th parallel.

### How did the UN react to the Chinese invasion of Korea during the Korean War?

In January 1951 the UN counter-attacked the Chinese and North Korean forces, pushing them back to the 38th parallel and retaking Seoul.

### What was the stalemate in the Korean War?

Between July 1951 and July 1953, while negotiations were ongoing, fighting continued along a fortified frontier near the 39th parallel. This cost many lives but gained little territory.

### Why was the Armistice signed in the Korean War?

In July 1953 an armistice was signed that agreed a border very similar to that of the 38th parallel. This was for a number of reasons.

- Eisenhower had replaced Truman as president and was keen to end the war.
- Stalin's death in 1953 made China and North Korea less confident.

### How many people were killed in the Korean War?

There were a number of costs to the Korean War:

- 30,000 American troops were killed.
- 4,500 UN troops from other countries were killed.
- Approximately 70,000 South Korean soldiers died.
- About 500,000 South Korean civilians were killed.
- An estimated 780,000 North Korean and Chinese soldiers and civilians died in the war.

### What was the fighting like in the Korean War?

The fighting in Korea took place in mountains, ravines and swamps - terrain that was more familiar to the Koreans and Chinese than the UN. They also had to contend with terrible cold and snowstorms in winter.

> **DID YOU KNOW?**
>
> **3 facts about the Korean War:**
> - The Korean War involved many different countries including the USSR, China, America and 21 countries fighting as a part of a UN force.
> - Korea is still divided today. The North is a communist dictatorship.
> - Korea is still technically at war as a peace treaty has never been signed.

# THE INVASION OF SOUTH KOREA

*'War is not only a contest of strength, but also a test of morality and ethics.' - Kim Il-Sung*

### What happened when North Korea invaded South Korea?

The Korean War *(p.37)* broke out when North Korea invaded South Korea and sent troops over the 38th parallel.

### When did North Korea invade South Korea?

North Korea invaded South Korea on 25th June, 1950.

### Why did North Korea invade South Korea?

North Korea invaded South Korea for 5 key reasons:

- North Korea invaded the south because Kim Il-Sung wanted to unite Korea under communist rule. By June 1950, he was confident an invasion would be successful.
- Kim Il-Sung had the support of communist leaders - Stalin in the USSR, and Mao Zedong in China.
- North Korea's armed forces were stronger than those of South Korea. The USSR had provided tanks, planes and heavy artillery.
- China became communist in 1949 and, after August that year, the USSR had the atom bomb. Kim Il-Sung thought these factors would deter a US response.
- American politicians had made speeches suggesting Korea was not seen as a priority.

### Why were North Korean troops able to invade South Korea so easily?

Very few American troops were available to help the South Koreans defend their territory, making it easier for the north to invade.

### What was the significance of North Korea's invasion of South Korea?

North Korea's invasion of South Korea was significant because it triggered a large-scale conflict that would last for 3 years and become the first hotspot of the Cold War in Asia.

### DID YOU KNOW?

**The Korean War is the name given to the conflict by the West.**
In North Korea, it is known as the Fatherland Liberation War, while in South Korea it is called Six-Two-Five because it began on 25th June.

# USA'S INVOLVEMENT WITH THE KOREAN WAR

*'It is fatal to enter an war without the will to win it.' - General Douglas MacArthur*

### What was America's response to the invasion of South Korea?

The USA put pressure on the United Nations to condemn the North Korean invasion *(p.41)*. It took control of the subsequent UN invasion and supplied by far the largest number of troops.

### Why did America defend South Korea during the invasion?

America had a number of reasons for wanting to defend South Korea, and for pressuring the UN to become involved:

- It had been involved in establishing the Republic of Korea.
- It was determined, under its policy of containment, to prevent further communist expansion.
- It was concerned the invasion of South Korea might encourage a Chinese attack on Formosa (Taiwan) and lead to a massive shift in world power from capitalism to communism.
- If the UN had failed to act, it is likely America would have taken action on its own to prevent this.
- Truman wanted to avoid the mistakes of the 1930s. There would be no appeasement and the USA would support the UN to ensure it did not fail as the League of Nations had.

### How was the UN influenced by America in the invasion of South Korea?

The United Nations' action in Korea was very much influenced by the USA.

- The UN forces were commanded by General MacArthur, an American.
- Half the ground forces were American.
- America contributed more than 90% of the air forces.
- 85% of the naval forces were American.

### Why did the USA's response to the invasion of South Korea lead to some people calling it 'America's war'?

Some people called the Korean War *(p.37)* 'America's war' for the following reasons:

- The amount of troops the USA sent to support UN forces - 302,483 soldiers in total. The UK sent the second highest number of troops, but that was only 14,198.
- An American, General MacArthur, led the UN army in Korea.
- It was widely known the forces took their orders from the USA rather than from the United Nations.

### DID YOU KNOW?

The Korean War was the first conflict to feature battles between jet aircraft.

*Quizzes, amazing exam preparation tools and more at GCSEHistory.com*

# GENERAL MACARTHUR AND THE KOREAN WAR

*'We hurled back the invader and decimated his forces. Our victory was complete, and our objectives within reach, when Red China intervened with numerically superior ground forces.' - General Douglas MacArthur*

### What did General Douglas MacArthur do in the Korean War?

At the age of 70, General Douglas MacArthur was appointed chief of the UN task force sent to Korea in 1950. He played a significant role in the Korean War *(p.37)*.

### What were the key events General Douglas MacArthur was involved in during the Korean War?

The 8 key events of MacArthur's role in the Korean War *(p.37)* included:

- When MacArthur arrived in Korea, his first job was to stop the South Korean army being completely wiped out. He sent troops to defend the area around the city of Pusan.
- MacArthur then launched a surprise attack, called the Inchon Landings.
- Next, he led UN forces to recapture the city of Seoul, which had fallen to Kim Il-Sung's North Korean army.
- By October 1950, MacArthur had successfully led the UN campaign to drive the North Korean army back to their homeland, behind the 38th parallel.
- MacArthur then launched an offensive into North Korea in the hope of reuniting Korea under capitalism. This went against recommendations not to do so, due to the concern China would join the war. However, MacArthur was confident Mao's troops would not attack.
- MacArthur's predictions were wrong, and he and his troops were pushed back into South Korea by the united force of North Korean and Chinese soldiers.
- MacArthur was ordered by Truman not to go back into North Korea. He ignored this, saying he wanted to unite Korea and the USA should be prepared to engage in nuclear warfare if this is what it took.
- As a result of disregarding President Truman's orders, MacArthur was sacked in April 1951 and ordered to return to the USA.

### Why was General Douglas MacArthur sacked during the Korean War?

MacArthur was sacked because he disobeyed direct orders. There was real concern he might trigger a nuclear war. Some people felt he deliberately provoked China into entering the war by ignoring their warnings against advancing further north in Korea. He also repeatedly expressed a willingness to use nuclear weapons.

### Who took over General Douglas MacArthur's role in the Korean War?

General MacArthur was replaced by Lieutenant General Matthew Ridgway.

### What was the public reaction to General Douglas MacArthur being sacked during the Korean War?

MacArthur was a popular war hero in America and his sacking was condemned by the public. He received a hero's welcome on his return home.

### What was the significance of General Douglas MacArthur's role during the Korean War?

MacArthur was a significant and controversial figure in the Korean War *(p.37)* for 5 main reasons:

- He was responsible for changing the tide of events, masterminding the Inchon Landing, and was able to recapture South Korea at the start of the war.
- His actions led to China's involvement, which turned the tide again - but this time not in the UN's favour.
- He was sacked by President Truman for disregarding orders and was replaced by Lieutenant General Ridgway.
- His attitude regarding nuclear warfare was heavily criticised. Some people felt there was a real danger of the conflict becoming a nuclear war and MacArthur was pushing towards this.
- He wrote a public letter criticising President Truman.

> **DID YOU KNOW?**
>
> General MacArthur fought in the First World War and won 13 medals for his acts of bravery.

# IMPACT OF THE KOREAN WAR

*'It will begin with its president taking a simple, firm resolution...to concentrate on the job of ending the war in Korea.' - General Eisenhower, 1952*

### How successful was American intervention in Korea?

The Korean War *(p.37)* fulfilled a number of US containment aims, but at a cost.

### How successful was American intervention in Korea?

The Korean War *(p.37)* was successful from the point of view of the US for a number of reasons.

- South Korea remained out of communist hands.
- The UN was shown to be more purposeful than the League of Nations had been, in using military sanctions to stop an act of aggression.
- It confirmed US policy in Asia and led to the setting up of SEATO.

### How was American intervention in Korea unsuccessful?

The success of the Korean War *(p.37)* was limited by a number of factors.

- It was costly in terms of life and money. The number of Americans who died per year was actually higher than during the Vietnam War.
- It failed to liberate North Korea from communism.
- It highlighted tension between American leaders, those who wanted to contain and prevent the spread of communism, and those who wanted to push back and win back communist countries.
- When China involved itself in the war it became a new major threat for the USA. Even after the fighting had stopped, US soldiers remained stationed in South Korea which irritated the Chinese government and put pressure on relations between the two countries.
- It had a devastating impact on the Korean people. Around a 10th of the population died.

> **DID YOU KNOW?**
>
> **The Korean War ended on 27th July, 1953, when an armistice was signed and a ceasefire agreed.**
>
> However, as of 2020, there has still never been a formal end to the conflict.

# PEACEFUL COEXISTENCE

*Peaceful coexistence did not mean the end of the Cold War.*

### What was peaceful coexistence?

In terms of the Cold War *(p.14)*, peaceful coexistence is the policy of accepting the existence of the other superpower so that both sides could exist without having to resort to war. It meant living in peace with each other, although competition between the two superpowers could continue.

### When was peaceful coexistence?

The period of peaceful coexistence occurred in the early 1950s.

### Who was responsible for peaceful coexistence?

Nikita Khrushchev, the leader of the USSR between 1953 and 1964, is associated with the policy of peaceful coexistence.

### Why was peaceful coexistence created?

There were 4 key reasons why Khrushchev supported the policy of peaceful coexistence:

- The USSR wanted to improve their relationship with the USA.
- Khrushchev believed that the USSR was superior to the USA. Communism would win in the end when the capitalist system collapsed, so there was little point in starting a war with the USA.
- The Korean War *(p.37)* ended in 1953 so the tension between the USSR and the USA was reducing.
- By reducing tension and accepting peaceful coexistence, it was hoped that spending on the arms race could be reduced.

### What happened during peaceful coexistence?

The 2 key events of peaceful coexistence were:

- An agreement between the USA, France, Britain and the USSR. They discussed how Austria should be ruled as Austria was still occupied after the Second World War.
- In the Geneva Summit, July 1955, the USSR, the USA, France and Britain discussed disarmament and Germany. Despite no formal agreements, the East-West relationship improved slightly.

### Why did peaceful coexistence end?

Peaceful coexistence ended for 3 key reasons:

- In May 1955, West Germany became a member of NATO *(p.34)* which greatly angered the USSR. The USSR created the Warsaw Pact *(p.35)* which increased tension.
- The USSR and the USA still competed in space.
- Khrushchev crushed the Hungarian Uprising *(p.47)* in 1956 which the West condemned.

---

**DID YOU KNOW?**

Khrushchev stated: 'I repeat, there is only one way to peace, one way out of the existing tension: peaceful coexistence.'

# DE-STALINISATION

*Khrushchev began the policy of de-Stalinisation after his 'Secret Speech' in which he criticised the brutality of Stalin's government.*

### What was De-Stalinisation?

De-Stalinisation was a series of political reforms in the USSR which were introduced after the death of Stalin in 1953.

### When did De-Stalinisation happen?

De-Stalinisation took place from 1956 to 1964.

### Who introduced De-Stalinisation?

Khrushchev brought in the policy of De-Stalinisation in his 'Secret Speech'.

### What did the 'Secret Speech' say about Stalin's government during the period of De-Stalinisation?

Khrushchev's 'Secret Speech' criticised the brutality of Stalin's government and led people to believe Soviet control would be relaxed in eastern Europe.

### Why was De-Stalinisation introduced?

There were 3 possible reasons why Khrushchev brought in his policy of De-Stalinisation:

- ✅ To weaken the position of his political rivals inside the USSR's Communist Party.
- ✅ To weaken the secret police and the Gulag system.
- ✅ To help develop peaceful coexistence *(p.45)* with the USA, with the idea the USSR would not interfere in America's affairs.

### What was the impact of De-Stalinisation on the Cold War?

De-Stalinisation influenced the Cold War *(p.14)* in 3 main ways:

- ✅ It was seen as a time when the relationship between the USA and the USSR improved - there was a 'thaw' in the Cold War *(p.14)*.
- ✅ When the contents of the 'Secret Speech' reached eastern Europe, people expected the repressive nature of communist-controlled governments would be relaxed.
- ✅ It encouraged rebellions in Hungary and, later, Czechoslovakia.

### What actions did De-Stalinisation lead to?

Khrushchev's programme of De-Stalinisation included the following 6 main actions:

- ✅ Cominform *(p.29)* was closed down.
- ✅ Soviet troops were withdrawn from Austria, where they had been since 1945.
- ✅ Marshall Tito of Yugoslavia was invited to Moscow.
- ✅ Thousands of political prisoners were released.
- ✅ Stalin's foreign minister, Molotov, was sacked.
- ✅ He seemed to promise greater freedom for the people of eastern Europe.

---

**DID YOU KNOW?**

The 'Secret Speech' soon leaked and led to demands for reform in eastern Europe.

# HUNGARIAN UPRISING, 1956

*'The 5,000 students who were meeting in front of the Petofi Monument in Budapest were joined shortly after dusk by thousands of workers and others. The great crowd then marched to the Stalin monument. Ropes were wound round the statue's neck, and, to cheers, the crowd attempted to topple the statue.' - The Manchester Guardian, 1956*

## What was the Hungarian Uprising?

The Hungarian people demonstrated against communist rule. Prime Minister Imre Nagy ended one-party rule and announced that Hungary would leave the Warsaw Pact *(p.35)*.

## When did the Hungarian Uprising happen?

The uprising in Hungary happened between July and October, 1956.

## Why did the Hungarian Uprising happen?

There were 4 main causes of the Hungarian Uprising:

- Since 1949 the USSR had taken industrial and agricultural goods away from Hungary, and as a result Hungary was very poor.
- Hungary's Prime Minister, Matyas Rakosi, was a hard-line communist and had crushed all political opposition in Hungary.
- Khrushchev, the new leader of the USSR, gave a secret speech in 1956 in which he criticised Stalin's brutality. Consequently, Hungarians hoped for more freedom.
- Living standards had fallen and people were suffering.

## What happened during the Hungarian Uprising?

There were 4 key events during the Hungarian Uprising:

- In July 1956, people began to protest about the repressive nature of the government and low standards of living.
- Rakosi was replaced by Gero as prime minister in the hope protests would decrease.
- In October 1956 there were huge protests by students and workers demanding more freedom which turned into riots.
- On 24th October, Nagy was appointed prime minister. He was more liberal and brought in reforms.

## What reforms did Nagy want to introduce during the Hungarian Uprising?

Nagy announced 5 key reforms, including:

- Relaxing censorship.
- Allowing free elections.
- Allowing non-communists into the government.
- A proposal for Hungary to withdraw from the Warsaw Pact *(p.35)*.
- The release of political prisoners, including Cardinal Jozsef Mindszenty who had been imprisoned by Rakosi.

## Why did the USSR invade Hungary during the Hungarian Uprising?

The USSR invaded Hungary because of Nagy's reforms and specifically because Nagy proposed that Hungary withdraw from the Warsaw Pact *(p.35)*.

## What happened as a consequence of the Hungarian Uprising?

There were 9 important consequences of the Hungarian Uprising:

- On 4th November, 1956, Khrushchev and the politburo ordered Soviet forces to invade Hungary with 200,000 troops to remove Nagy and crush the uprising.

- Between 20,000 and 30,000 Hungarians were killed.
- 1,000 Soviet troops died.
- 200,000 Hungarians became refugees.
- Nagy's government was deported, and Nagy was executed.
- Nagy was replaced by Janos Kadar and a new pro-Communist government loyal to the USSR was set up.
- All Nagy's reforms were reversed.
- This was used as a warning to other dissenting (protesting) countries in eastern Europe.
- It increased tension between the West and the East.

### What was the response of the West to the Hungarian Uprising?

The West responded in 4 key ways:
- The United Nations condemned the Soviet actions.
- Spain, the Netherlands and Switzerland boycotted the 1956 Olympics.
- America accepted 80,000 refugees from Hungary.
- The USA could not send troops to help Hungary because the Warsaw Pact *(p.35)* would see it as an invasion and war would break out.

### What did the new government do after the Hungarian Uprising?

The new Hungarian government, under Janos Kadar, remained under Soviet control and reacted in 3 key ways:
- It stamped out remaining resistance. 35,000 Hungarian protesters were arrested and 300 executed.
- A few of the reforms demanded by the Hungarians were introduced, cautiously.
- Kadar remained firmly in favour of Hungary's membership of the Warsaw Pact *(p.35)*.

### What was the importance of the Hungarian Uprising?

The Hungarian Uprising was important because it affected the relationship between the USA and the USSR in 3 key ways:
- The USA supported the uprising but could not interfere, so now looked weak.
- Khrushchev's position was strengthened as a result.
- The USSR and the USA's relationship deteriorated because the USA had condemned the USSR's actions, increasing tension.

---

**DID YOU KNOW?**

The crushing of the 1956 uprising by the Soviets caused several famous members of communist parties around the world to leave in disgust.

# BERLIN CRISIS, 1958-61

*The Berlin Crisis was the culmination of conflict between the USSR and USA over the future of Germany.*

### What was the Berlin Crisis?

The Berlin Crisis concerned the occupational status of the city and the numbers of East Germans fleeing to West Berlin, said to be some 2.7 million people. Khrushchev delivered an ultimatum, demanding foreign troops withdraw within a period of 6 months.

### When did the Berlin Crisis happen?

The Berlin Crisis took place between 1957 and 1961.

### Why did people move to West Berlin during the Berlin Crisis?

For many East Germans, life in the West seemed more attractive for 3 key reasons:

- Wages were higher in West Berlin.
- West Berliners had more freedom and more variety in the goods that they could buy.
- The Allies poured money into West Berlin, so that the contrast between the affluence of the city's two sides was more obvious.

### How was the economy affected during the Berlin Crisis?

The West German economy benefitted from skilled labourers, while the East suffered a skills shortage.

### What were the key events of the Berlin Crisis?

There were 8 key events during the Berlin Crisis:

- In 1958 the leader of East Germany, Walter Ulbricht, asked Khrushchev, the leader of the USSR, to help stop East Germans from fleeing to the west.
- In November 1958, Khrushchev issued his ultimatum demanding Western troops withdraw from West Berlin.
- In 1959, Khrushchev and President Eisenhower met in Geneva to discuss the Berlin Crisis, which resulted in Khrushchev withdrawing his ultimatum.
- A second summit, at Camp David in America in 1959, did not result in a solution.
- In 1960, a US spy plane was shot down by the Soviets.
- President Eisenhower refused to apologise for the U2 spy plane so Khrushchev left the Paris Conference of 1960. Again, this meant no solution was found to the Berlin Crisis.
- In 1961, the US and the USSR met again in Vienna. Khrushchev reissued his ultimatum for the Western powers to withdraw their troops from Berlin within 6 months.
- President Kennedy *(p.70)* began to prepare for war, increasing American defence spending by $3.5 billion. The USSR did the same.

### What were the results of the Berlin Crisis?

There were 6 key results:

- East German troops began to build the Berlin Wall *(p.50)* on 13th August, 1961.
- By October 1961 West Berlin was entirely shut off from East Germany. Initially, foreigners could cross into East Berlin through a US Army checkpoint, known as Checkpoint Charlie.
- It reduced tension as the crisis was solved without going to war.
- French, British and American troops remained in West Berlin.
- It was a propaganda victory for the West and a humiliation for the USSR, because the East had to build a wall to prevent its people fleeing.

- As the USSR had been humiliated, Khrushchev became more determined to win the Cuban Missile Crisis *(p.54)* in 1962.

> **DID YOU KNOW?**
> The flight of East German refugees to the West is often referred to as a 'brain drain' because those who fled were mainly well-educated professionals.

## THE BERLIN WALL, 1961-62

*The Berlin Wall is perhaps the first symbol that comes to mind when people think of the Cold War - a physical wall separating capitalism and communism in the same city.*

### What was the Berlin Wall?

The Berlin Wall, built by East Germany, divided East and West Berlin. It was constructed of concrete slabs in the city centre and barbed wire fences around the outer edges.

### When was the Berlin Wall built?

The building of the Berlin Wall began on the 12th-13th August, 1961.

### Why was the Berlin Wall built?

There were 2 main reasons for the building of the Berlin Wall:

- To prevent East German people defecting to West Berlin.
- To keep capitalism and spies from the West out, according to the Soviets and East German government.

### What were the consequences of the Berlin Wall being built?

There were 7 key consequences of the building of the Berlin Wall:

- It solved the refugee crisis for East Germany, which now controlled who could leave and enter East Berlin.
- West Berlin remained under Allied control, making it harder for the Soviets to control the whole of East Germany.
- The number of military alerts in Berlin decreased as the situation there became less tense.
- It was a humiliation for the USSR and a propaganda victory for the West, as it appeared a wall was needed to prevent people fleeing.
- It divided West Berliners from East Berliners. Families and friends were separated for years.
- At least 140 people died attempting to cross the Berlin Wall from the east to the west between 1961 and 1989; some reports say the figure was higher.
- It became an iconic symbol of the Cold War *(p.14)*.

### What was President Kennedy's response to the building of the Berlin Wall?

President Kennedy's *(p.70)* responded in 2 main ways:

- He said: 'It's not a very nice solution but a wall is a hell of a lot better than a war.'.
- He visited West Berlin in June 1963, where he gave the 'Ich bin ein Berliner' speech to show his support for West Berliners.

### What was the impact of the Berlin Wall on the relationship between the USA and the USSR?

There were both positive and negative effects on the relationship between the USA and the USSR:

- It solved the crisis over Berlin so reduced tension.
- There were fewer military alerts in Berlin as the situation had stabilised.
- Germany had been a source of conflict between the USSR and the USA since 1945. Their relationship had deteriorated so much a wall had to be built.
- It created a long-lasting symbol of the Cold War *(p.14)* which signified the divide between the two sides.
- Khrushchev had suffered a humiliating defeat so decided to place missiles in Cuba to show he could stand up to the USA.
- Khrushchev saw Kennedy *(p.70)* as weak as he had not stopped the wall from being built.

### What happened at Checkpoint Charlie after the Berlin Wall was built?

Two main points should be noted about what happened at Checkpoint Charlie:

- There was an 18-hour standoff when Soviet tanks stopped Americans crossing the border on 27th-28th October, 1961.
- It was a high point of tension between East and West until an agreement between the USA and USSR ended the incident.

> **DID YOU KNOW?**
> A trapeze artist called Horst Klein managed to escape over the Berlin Wall by tightrope-walking across a power line in 1962. He fell and broke both his arms, but landed in West Berlin.

# CUBAN REVOLUTION, 1959

*'A revolution is not a bed of roses. A revolution is a struggle to the death between the future and the past.' - Fidel Castro*

### What was the Cuban Revolution?

Fidel Castro led an armed uprising to bring down the dictatorship of the Cuban president, General Fulgencio Batista.

### When was the Cuban Revolution?

The Cuban Revolution started in July 1953. Batista was removed from power on 31st December, 1958.

### Who started the Cuban Revolution?

Fidel Castro started the Cuban Revolution.

### How did the Cuban Revolution affect Cuba's relationship with the USA?

Before 1959, the USA supported Batista and there was co-operation between the two countries. This ended when diplomatic relations were broken off in January 1961.

### What was the USA's reaction to the Cuban Revolution?

The USA reacted in 7 key ways:

- It wanted Cuba back inside America's sphere of influence.

- In 1959, it refused to accept compensation offered by Cuba for American-owned property and land taken in the revolution.
- Although America did recognise Castro's government, when he requested economic aid in 1960 this was denied. Instead, President Eisenhower reduced US imports of Cuban sugar by 95%.
- It supported Cuban exiles to undermine the new government.
- It refused to buy Cuban sugar, which made up a large part of the national income, and eventually ended all trade with Cuba in October 1960.
- The CIA tried unsuccessfully to assassinate Castro.
- The CIA convinced President Kennedy *(p.70)* that the USA needed to invade Cuba.

### What became of Cuba's relationship with the USSR after the Cuban Revolution?

There were 3 important developments in Cuba's relationship with the Soviet Union:
- Cuba began to build economic links with the Soviet Union instead of the USA.
- In February 1960, it began to trade Cuban sugar for Soviet oil.
- Cuba wanted the Soviets' military defence and support.

---

**DID YOU KNOW?**

The Communist Party still rules in Cuba today.

---

# U2 CRISIS

*The US spy plane incident was a major embarrassment for the USA.*

### What was the U2 Crisis?
The U2 Crisis happened when the Soviet Union shot down a U2 American spy plane.

### What happened in the U2 Crisis?
The 4 key events in the story of the U2 Crisis are:
- US pilot Gary Powers flew a U2 spy plane over the Soviet Union to spy on its military capabilities.
- Khrushchev ordered the spy plane to be shot down and Powers was arrested and put on trial as a spy.
- The USA tried to claim it was only a weather plane, but the Soviets produced clear evidence it was a spy plane.
- Gary Powers was jailed for ten years by the Soviets.

### When was the U2 crisis?
The U2 Crisis happened on 1st May, 1960.

### What was the impact of the U2 crisis?
The U2 Crisis had 3 main consequences.
- Khrushchev stormed out of the Paris Peace Conference in 1960.
- The idea of the 'thaw' in tensions created during de-Stalinisation *(p.46)* was over. Tensions were now high again.
- President Kennedy *(p.70)* promised to be tougher on communism.

### DID YOU KNOW?

**3 facts about the U2 Spy Plane incident:**
- ✓ Gary Powers, the pilot, went on trial in the USSR and was sentenced to 10 years in jail.
- ✓ Secretly, the US and the USSR negotiated a prisoner swap. Gary Powers was exchanged for a Russian spy called Rudolf Abel.
- ✓ The two men were 'swapped' on Glienicke Bridge in Berlin.

# BAY OF PIGS, 1961

*The Bay of Pigs was one of the most catastrophic foreign policy interventions in American history.*

### What happened at the Bay of Pigs in Cuba?
The Bay of Pigs incident involved Cuban exiles, supported by US forces, invading Cuba.

### When was the attack at the Bay of Pigs?
The invasion of Cuba at the Bay of Pigs took place on 17th April, 1961.

### Who led the attack at the Bay of Pigs?
Cuban exiles, trained and supported by America, invaded Cuba at the Bay of Pigs.

### What happened during the invasion of the Bay of Pigs?
There were 4 key events during the invasion of the Bay of Pigs:
- ☑ Castro learned about the invasion in advance because the planes were recognised as American from photographs.
- ☑ The 1,400 US-backed Cuban exiles were met by an army of 20,000 Cubans.
- ☑ The US-backed Cuban exiles surrendered.
- ☑ Almost all of those in the Cuban exile army were jailed or shot.

### What were the consequences of the attack at the Bay of Pigs?
There were 5 important consequences of the attack at the Bay of Pigs:
- ☑ The incident meant USA-Cuban relations deteriorated while Soviet-Cuban relations improved.
- ☑ Fidel Castro stayed in power.
- ☑ The USA was totally discredited because it had supported illegal acts. President Kennedy *(p.70)* was embarrassed and his position was weakened.
- ☑ In December 1961, Castro stated he and his government were communist.
- ☑ Castro asked Khrushchev for military support in case of future attacks by the USA.

### Why did the invasion at the Bay of Pigs fail?
There were 2 main reasons why the invasion at the Bay of Pigs failed:
- ☑ The CIA underestimated the strength of the Cubans, who had 20,000 troops and modern tanks and weapons.
- ☑ They also failed to gain the support of the Cuban people, which they assumed they would get.

> **DID YOU KNOW?**
>
> **The failure of the Bay of Pigs invasion had several consequences.**
>
> President Kennedy was humiliated, and there were a number of failed attempts by the CIA to assassinate Fidel Castro.

# CUBAN MISSILE CRISIS, OCTOBER 1962

*'We're eyeball to eyeball...and I think the other fellow just blinked.' - Secretary of State Dean Rusk, October 1962*

### What was the Cuban Missile Crisis?

The Cuban Missile Crisis, between the USSR and the USA, was one of the most serious Cold War *(p.14)* crises. It happened because the USSR placed missiles in Cuba and was the closest the world had been to a possible nuclear war.

### When did the Cuban Missile Crisis happen?

The Cuban Missile Crisis lasted for 13 days, from 14th to 28th October, 1962.

### Why did the Cuban Missile Crisis happen?

6 important causes of the Cuban Missile Crisis were:

- The long-term deterioration of the relationship between the USA and Cuba, accelerated by the Cuban Revolution *(p.51)* in 1959 and the Bay of Pigs incident in 1961.
- This pushed Cuba closer to the USSR, which bought Cuban sugar. In return, the Cubans bought oil from the Soviets.
- Castro had declared himself a Marxist in December 1961.
- Khrushchev was concerned about the missile gap and the fact the USA had nuclear missiles based in Turkey which could easily reach the USSR.
- The immediate cause was the deployment of Soviet nuclear missiles to Cuba for protection against possible attack by the USA.
- Cuba is only 160km south of the US state of Florida, which meant the mainland was within range of any missiles placed on Cuba. The USA therefore felt threatened.

### What happened during the Cuban Missile Crisis?

There were 9 key events during the crisis in October 1962:

- On 14th October, American spy planes spotted missile bases being built on Cuba.
- On 16th October, Kennedy *(p.70)* was informed of the missile build-up and Ex-Comm, an advisory group, was formed.
- On 20th October, Kennedy *(p.70)* decided to blockade Cuba. This was a 500-mile naval 'quarantine' with the aim of preventing the Soviets bringing in further military supplies or missiles.
- On 24th October, Khrushchev stated the USSR would launch nuclear missiles if America went to war in Cuba.
- The blockade began. When Soviet ships approached the blockade, some stopped and some turned around.
- On 26th October, Kennedy *(p.70)* received a letter from Khrushchev who offered to negotiate if the blockade was removed and the USA did not invade Cuba.
- On 27th October, Kennedy *(p.70)* received a second letter from Khrushchev which offered to remove the missiles if the USA removed its missiles in Turkey.

*Quizzes, amazing exam preparation tools and more at GCSEHistory.com*

- Kennedy's *(p.70)* brother, Robert, negotiated with the Russian ambassador and accepted the offer on condition the removal of missiles from Turkey was kept secret.
- On 28th October, Khrushchev agreed to the dismantling of the nuclear missiles.

## How was the Cuban Missile Crisis solved?

The Cuban Missile Crisis was solved because:

- Khrushchev agreed to remove missiles from Cuba if the USA removed its warheads from Italy and Turkey.
- The USA would only agree to the deal if the removal of its missiles from Italy and Turkey was kept secret.

## What were the results of the Cuban Missile Crisis?

There were 6 main consequences to the Cuban Missile Crisis:

- Cuba survived as a communist country.
- Kennedy *(p.70)* assured the world that the USA would never invade Cuba and his public image improved.
- The Soviet Union looked weak because the world did not know the USA had removed its missiles from Turkey.
- Khrushchev lost power in the USSR and was dismissed in 1964.
- China criticised the USSR over its actions because the Soviets had made the communist world look weak. China's relationship with the USSR deteriorated.
- The USA's NATO *(p.34)* allies in Europe were horrified because they had not been consulted. France reacted by leaving NATO in 1966.

## How did the Cuban Missile Crisis affect the relationship between the USA and the USSR?

The Cuban Missile Crisis had 2 main effects on the relationship between the USA and the USSR:

- The relationship had deteriorated almost to the brink of nuclear war, so Kennedy *(p.70)* wanted to focus more on the two nations' 'common interests'.
- A hotline *(p.62)* was set up in June 1963 between the USA and the USSR. This would help avoid crises by enabling direct and quick communication.

## Why was the Cuban Missile Crisis important?

The Cuban Missile Crisis was important for 2 main reasons:

- It was the most dangerous Cold War *(p.14)* confrontation between the USA and the USSR and almost led to nuclear war.
- It resulted in both countries working to improve their relationship and slow down the arms race.

## What nuclear treaties were signed after The Cuban Missile Crisis?

There were 3 important nuclear treaties signed after the Cuban Missile Crisis:

- 1963 - the Limited Test Ban Treaty *(p.63)* banned the testing of nuclear weapons in air or underwater.
- 1967 - the Outer Space Treaty *(p.64)* banned testing or using nuclear weapons in space.
- 1968 - the Nuclear Non-Proliferation Treaty stated the ultimate goal was world nuclear disarmament.

---

**DID YOU KNOW?**

**One man, Vasili Arkhipov, is credited with 'saving the world' by refusing to fire nuclear missiles during the crisis.**

His actions may have prevented an all-out nuclear war as the crisis is often seen as the closest the human race has ever come to self-annihilation; both superpowers were ready to resort to a potentially nuclear war

# PRAGUE SPRING, 1968

*'In twenty years, not one human problem has been solved in our country.' - Czech Ludvik Vaculik, 1968*

### What was the Prague Spring?

The Prague Spring is the term used for the brief period when the government of Czechoslovakia wanted to democratise the nation and reduce the control the USSR had on the country.

### When was the Prague Spring?

The Prague Spring took place between 5th January and 21st August in 1968.

### Who was responsible for the Prague Spring?

Alexander Dubček, the new leader of Czechoslovakia, introduced the reforms.

### What were the causes of the Prague Spring?

There were 6 main reasons for the Prague Spring.

- Since 1957, Czechoslovakia had been led by Antonin Novotný, who was very unpopular because he was a hard-line communist.
- Novotný did not bring in reforms, despite Khrushchev's de-Stalinisation *(p.46)* policy.
- By the 1960s, the Czech economy was struggling, and the standard of living was decreasing.
- When the leader of the USSR, Brezhnev, visited Czechoslovakia in December 1967, he withdrew his support for Novotný because he was so unpopular.
- Novotný was replaced by Dubček as the leader of Czechoslovakia on 5th January, 1968, in the hope that this would reduce discontent.
- Dubček wanted to reform communism to create 'socialism with a human face'. This would enable the public to be more involved in the government and, hopefully, increase support for communism.

### What were the reforms of the Prague Spring introduced by Dubček?

Dubček brought in 7 main reforms.

- Censorship was relaxed in April 1968, which allowed more criticism of communism.
- Free speech was allowed.
- Political parties other than the Communist Party were allowed to exist.
- Work councils were set up to represent workers and improve working conditions.
- The secret police had their powers restricted, so their ability to arrest and detain people without trial was reduced.
- Some capitalist elements were even allowed, to create a form of 'market socialism' economy.
- Travel restrictions were lifted, so Czechs could travel abroad.

### What was the response from the Czechoslovakian Communist Party to the Prague Spring?

The response from the leaders of the Czechoslovakian Communist Party was not enthusiastic.

- Many were horrified at Dubček's reforms, believing they were a threat to communism.
- On 3rd August, 1968, 5 leading opponents of the Prague Spring reforms sent a letter to Brezhnev, outlining their concerns and asking him to intervene.

### Why were Eastern Bloc leaders concerned during the Prague Spring?

Brezhnev, the leader of the USSR, and Erich Honecker, the leader of East Germany, were very worried for 3 main reasons.

- Romania would not attend Warsaw Pact *(p.35)* meetings.
- Tito, the leader of Yugoslavia, did not want the USSR to control his country.
- They feared the Prague Spring would lead to calls for reform elsewhere in the Soviet Union's sphere of influence.

## What was Brezhnev's response to the Prague Spring?

Brezhnev and the Eastern Bloc responded in 12 main ways.

- In July 1968, the USSR claimed to know of plans by West Germany to invade the Sudetenland, and asked to send Soviet troops to protect Czechoslovakia. Dubček refused.
- The USSR considered economic sanctions for Czechoslovakia, but didn't want the country to seek help from the West.
- In July, the entire Soviet Politburo (cabinet) visited Czechoslovakia, to put pressure on Dubček to reverse the reforms.
- Warsaw Pact *(p.35)* troops from the USSR, Poland and East Germany completed manoeuvres in Czechoslovakia in the summer, to put more pressure on Dubček.
- On 15th July, members of the Warsaw Pact *(p.35)* sent a letter to Dubček, warning him that the reforms were dangerous to the Eastern Bloc.
- On 20th-21st August, 1968, 500,000 Soviet-led Warsaw Pact *(p.35)* troops entered Prague to arrest the reformers.
- Nobody in Czechoslovakia was expecting an invasion, especially their armed troops, who were completely unprepared.
- Dubček and other leaders were arrested. They were taken to Moscow to meet Brezhnev.
- Dubček was forced to sign the Moscow Protocol, which stated that Czechoslovakia would protect communism and the reforms would be reversed.
- All the reforms were reversed when Dubček returned to Czechoslovakia.
- In August 1968, the Brezhnev Doctrine *(p.59)* was created. The USSR had the right to invade any country in its sphere of influence which threatened the stability of eastern Europe.
- The USSR wanted to ensure it had full control over Czechoslovakia. In 1969, therefore, it replaced Dubček with Husak, a hard-line and reliable communist.

## What was the reaction of the West to the Prague Spring and the Soviet invasion?

The West reacted in 3 key ways.

- The UN wanted to condemn the invasion of Czechoslovakia by Warsaw Pact *(p.35)* troops, but the USSR vetoed it.
- The USA and the West condemned the invasion.
- However, the USA did nothing because it was distracted by Vietnam, there was a US presidential election, and it was the beginning of détente. *(p.60)*

## What was the reaction of the communist world to the Prague Spring and the Soviet invasion?

The communist world reacted in 5 main ways.

- Communists in western countries condemned the invasion, and created their own version of communism called Eurocommunism.
- In France and Italy, the Communist Party condemned the USSR's actions.
- Yugoslavia and Romania spoke out against the USSR's invasion, which worsened their relationship with the Soviet Union.
- Poland and East Germany were very supportive of the invasion, as they were trying to control reformers in their own countries.
- Communist China condemned the USSR invasion of Czechoslovakia, and the relationship between the two countries greatly deteriorated.

## What was the importance of the Prague Spring?

The Prague Spring and the invasion by Soviet troops were important for 3 key reasons.

- They led to the creation of the Brezhnev Doctrine *(p.59)*, which increased USSR control over eastern Europe.
- It split the communist world, as communist parties in western Europe became independent of the USSR's control, and communist China condemned the invasion.
- It highlighted that, while the USA would condemn the USSR's actions, it wouldn't take any steps to stop them.

> **DID YOU KNOW?**
>
> 137 Czechoslovaks were killed resisting the Soviet invasion.

# DUBČEK

*'I have worked for thirty years in the Party, and my whole family has devoted everything to the affairs of the Party, the affairs of socialism. Let whatever is going to happen to me happen. I'm expecting the worst for myself and I'm resigned to it.' - Alexander Dubček*

### Who was Dubček?

Alexander Dubček was a leader of Czechoslovakia. He had a good relationship with Soviet leader Leonid Brezhnev, supported the Warsaw Pact *(p.35)* and wanted to introduce reforms to improve people's lives.

### When was Dubček in power?

Alexander Dubček was the leader of Czechoslovakia from January 1968 to August 1968.

### What were Dubček reforms called?

Dubček introduced reforms known as the Prague Spring *(p.56)* to create 'socialism with a human face'.

### What reforms did Dubček introduce?

There were 4 main reforms introduced by Dubček:

- He relaxed censorship.
- Other political parties were also permitted.
- The secret police had their powers reduced.
- Some capitalist elements were even allowed to create a form of "market socialism" economy.

### What happened to Dubček afterwards?

The following happened to Dubček:

- Dubček was arrested and forced to visit Moscow.
- He was ordered to reverse all his reforms.
- In 1969, Dubček was replaced by Husak, who was a hardline communist Moscow could rely on.
- He was appointed Ambassador to Turkey until he was expelled from the party, and then he worked in forest administration.

> **DID YOU KNOW?**
>
> Dubček believed Lenin, the first leader of the Soviet Union, had been wrong about some things and that allowing elements of capitalism was necessary.

# BREZHNEV DOCTRINE, 1968

*'When forces that are hostile to socialism try to turn the development of some socialist country towards capitalism, it becomes not only a problem of the country concerned, but a common problem and concern of all socialist countries.' - Brezhnev Doctrine, 1968*

### What was the Brezhnev Doctrine?

The Brezhnev Doctrine stated that the USSR had the right to invade any country in its sphere of influence which threatened the stability of eastern Europe.

### Who was behind the Brezhnev Doctrine?

Leonid Brezhnev, the leader of the USSR between 1964 and 1982, created the Brezhnev Doctrine.

### Why was the Brezhnev Doctrine introduced?

Brezhnev introduced the Brezhnev Doctrine after the Prague Spring *(p.56)* because he realised he could not allow reforms in other eastern European nations.

### When was the Brezhnev Doctrine created?

The Brezhnev Doctrine was created in September 1968.

### How did the West react to the Brezhnev Doctrine?

The West reacted to the Brezhnev Doctrine in 3 main ways:

- It was condemned by the USA.
- Communist parties in the democratic west were shocked and broke away from the Soviet Communist Party to create their own version of communism, called Eurocommunism.
- It was condemned by the UN.

### How did the communists react to the Brezhnev Doctrine?

Other communist states reacted in the 3 main ways to the Brezhnev Doctrine:

- Communist governments in East Germany and Poland welcomed it because they were attempting to control reformers in their own countries.
- Romania and Yugoslavia were horrified and tried to distance themselves from the USSR and be more independent.
- China was angered and insulted by the Brezhnev Doctrine, as it only gave the USSR the right to intervene. Their relationship deteriorated.

### What was the significance of the Brezhnev Doctrine for eastern Europe?

Countries in the eastern European bloc now had to obey strict Soviet rule or risk invasion.

**DID YOU KNOW?**

Brezhnev enjoyed receiving medals so much he awarded himself 100 of them while he was in power.

# DÉTENTE

*'One has to be broad-minded and tolerant enough to understand the possibility and the desirability of coexistence and cooperation between nations that are vastly different in their social systems, political institutions, values, sympathies and antipathies.' - Georgi Arbatov, Soviet Central committee member, 1983*

### What was détente?

Détente refers to a period during the Cold War *(p.14)* where tensions between the USA and the Soviet Union were eased. There was increased cooperation and several attempts were made to slow down the arms race.

### When did détente happen?

Détente was between 1967 and 1979.

### What role did Henry Kissinger play in détente?

Henry Kissinger was very important to détente in 3 key ways:

- As President Nixon's security advisor, he organised Nixon's trips to Moscow and China in 1972.
- He also played an important role in the SALT 1 *(p.65)* talks.
- As Secretary of State, Kissinger helped end the Vietnam War for which he jointly received the Nobel Peace Prize in 1973.

### Why was the policy of détente introduced?

Détente occurred for 7 key reasons:

- Both the USSR and the USA wanted to ease tensions after the Cuban Missile Crisis *(p.54)* because they came so close to nuclear war.
- The Sino-Soviet relationship had deteriorated and the USSR wanted to prevent the USA becoming closer to China. The Soviets were worried when President Nixon visited China in 1972.
- Brezhnev, the leader of the USSR, wanted an improved relationship with the USA as he wanted access to US technology and grain.
- Both sides wanted to slow down the arms race because it was very expensive and they needed the money for domestic issues.
- The USA had domestic problems with anti-Vietnam War demonstrations, race riots and massive social inequality. It needed to cut defence spending so it could invest at home.
- The USSR had economic problems and needed to cut defence spending so there was money to invest at home.
- The USA needed the USSR's help to end the Vietnam War as they were supplying the Vietnamese communists. To find a solution, the USA asked the USSR for help.

### What were the key events of détente?

The 9 key events of détente were:

- ✓ 1968: Nuclear Non-Proliferation Treaty.
- ✓ 1970: Relations between East Germany and West Germany improved with the policy of Ostpolitik.
- ✓ 1970: Ostpolitik resulted in the Treaty of Warsaw, which recognised the existing borders between the countries.
- ✓ 1972: SALT 1 *(p.65)*.
- ✓ 1972: President Nixon visited China to meet Chairman Mao and visited Brezhnev in Moscow.
- ✓ 1972: Ostpolitik continued with the signing of the Basic Treaty which established formal relations between the two German nations.
- ✓ 1973: Brezhnev, leader of the USSR, visited Washington to meet Nixon.
- ✓ 1975: Helsinki Accords and the Apollo-Soyuz Missions.
- ✓ 1979: SALT 2.

### What role did Ostpolitik play in détente?

Ostpolitik was the policy of Chancellor Willy Brandt of West Germany which aimed to reduce tensions between the two German nations.

### What was the importance of détente?

The move towards détente led to the signing of the Strategic Arms Limitation Treaties, or SALT. These treaties were intended to limit the arms race in strategic ballistic missiles armed with nuclear weapons.

### Why did détente end?

The main reason détente ended was due to the USSR's invasion of Afghanistan in December 1979.

---

**DID YOU KNOW?**

The word 'détente' is French and means 'easing of tension.'

---

# CHINA AND DÉTENTE

*As the Sino-Soviet relationship deteriorated, the Sino-American relationship improved.*

### What about China and détente?

China played an important role in the period of détente *(p.60)*. The relationship between China and America improved. However, the relationship between China and the USSR grew more tense.

### When did China become involved with détente?

China's role in détente *(p.60)* occurred in the 1970s.

### What was China's relationship with the USA before détente?

America and China's relationship before détente *(p.60)* was tense because of 4 main reasons:

- ✓ Chairman Mao, the leader of China, did not trust America.
- ✓ Tensions increased when China joined the Korean War *(p.37)* on the side of North Korea in 1949. America supported South Korea.

- ✓ The relationship deteriorated again when America said in 1954 and 1958 it was prepared to use force to protect Taiwan from Chinese interference.
- ✓ In the 1960s Mao's followers publicly criticised the USA and called them 'capitalist running dogs' as an insult.

### What were the reasons for China being involved with détente?

There were 3 reasons why China became involved in détente *(p.60)*:

- ✓ China's relationship with the USSR had deteriorated.
- ✓ Both China and America viewed the USSR as a rival.
- ✓ The World Table Tennis championship was held in Japan in April 1971 and the Chinese and American teams became friendly which improved the diplomatic relationship.

### How did China's relationship with the USSR affect détente?

China's relationship with the USSR had deteriorated which pushed them towards the USA due to 5 key reasons:

- ✓ In 1950 Chairman Mao of China visited Stalin. They signed the Sino-Soviet Treaty of Friendship, Alliance and Mutual assistance, but Mao felt that China had not been respected.
- ✓ The Sino-Soviet relationship deteriorated further when Stalin died in 1953 because Mao disliked Khrushchev's policy of de-Stalinisation *(p.46)*.
- ✓ Khrushchev criticised Mao's policies in response.
- ✓ The relationship was seriously strained, when Mao accused Khrushchev of cowardice in Cuba and condemned the USSR's invasion of Czechoslovakia.
- ✓ The relationship hit an all time low, when fighting broke out on their border in 1969.

### What were the consequences of China being involved in détente?

There were 2 key impacts:

- ✓ Henry Kissinger, the Secretary of State for the USA, visited China in 1971 and met with the Prime Minister, Zhou Enlai.
- ✓ In 1972, Kissinger and Nixon signed the Shanghai Communique agreeing a peaceful outcome to the Taiwan question but acknowledging Taiwan was part of China.

---

**DID YOU KNOW?**

During this period of détente between China and the USA, there were a number of visits to each country.

This was called 'ping-pong diplomacy' because of the impact of the Table Tennis Championship in improving their relationship.

---

# HOTLINE, 1963

*'Must a world be lost for want of a telephone call?' - Jess Gorkin, 1960*

### What was the hotline?

The hotline was a teleprinter set up between Washington in the USA and Moscow in the USSR as a way of providing direct communication between the White House and the Kremlin.

## When was the hotline set up?

The hotline was set up in June 1963.

## Why was the hotline set up?

The hotline was set up as a result of the 1962 Cuban Missile Crisis (p.54). Leaders of the USA and the USSR had been unable to communicate directly during the crisis, relying on letters and messages.

## Why was the hotline important?

The hotline was important for 2 main reasons:

- ✅ It meant the USA and USSR could directly communicate with each other so in a crisis they would hopefully solve the issue more quickly.
- ✅ It was a sign that the two superpowers were attempting to improve their relationship.

> **DID YOU KNOW?**
>
> The hotline has never been a telephone, as depicted in some movies.
>
> Lyndon B Johnson was the first president to use the hotline, in 1967 during the Six Day War in the Middle East.

# TEST BAN TREATY, 1963

*The Limited Test Ban Treaty was the first attempt to slow down the arms race.*

## What was the Limited Test Ban Treaty?

The Limited Nuclear Test Ban Treaty banned the testing of nuclear weapons underwater, in the atmosphere or in outer space.

## When was the Limited Test Ban Treaty signed?

The Limited Nuclear Test Ban Treaty was signed on 5th August, 1963.

## Who signed the Limited Test Ban Treaty?

The USA, USSR and Great Britain signed the Limited Nuclear Test Ban Treaty.

## Why was the Limited Test Ban Treaty important?

The Limited Test Ban Treaty was seen as an important first step in slowing down the arms race by controlling the development of nuclear weapons.

> **DID YOU KNOW?**
>
> The USSR and the USA were so concerned about how close they had come to nuclear war during the Cuban Missile Crisis that both nations were prepared to put some limits on the arms race.

# OUTER SPACE TREATY, 1967

*The Outer Space Treaty prevents space being weaponised.*

### What was the Outer Space Treaty?
The Outer Space Treaty was an agreement to not deploy nuclear weapons in space or on any other space body, or to station them in outer space. The moon would be used for peaceful purposes only.

### When was the Outer Space Treaty signed?
The Outer Space Treaty was signed on 27th January, 1967.

### Who signed the Outer Space Treaty?
The Outer Space Treaty was signed by the USA, USSR and Britain.

### Why was the Outer Space Treaty important?
The Outer Space Treaty sets out the basic legal framework for international space law. It prevented the arms race from spreading to space.

> **DID YOU KNOW?**
>
> The terms of the Outer Space Treaty would have been broken by President Reagan's SDI programme.

# NUCLEAR NON-PROLIFERATION TREATY, 1968

*The Nuclear Non-Proliferation Treaty, 1968, essentially addressed the issue of giving away nuclear secrets.*

### What was the Non-Proliferation of Nuclear Weapons Treaty?
The countries that signed the Non-Proliferation of Nuclear Weapons Treaty agreed to stop the spread of nuclear weapons by not sharing their nuclear technology with other countries. The treaty is also known as the Non-Proliferation Treaty or NPT.

### When was the Non-Proliferation of Nuclear Weapons Treaty signed?
The Non-Proliferation of Nuclear Weapons Treaty was signed on 1st July, 1968.

### Who signed the Non-Proliferation of Nuclear Weapons Treaty?
The NPT was signed by the Soviet Union, the United Kingdom, and the United States.

> **DID YOU KNOW?**
>
> **The 50th anniversary of the Nuclear Non-Proliferation Treaty was on 5th March, 2020.**
>
> It opened for signature in 1968 and was put into force in 1970. The Treaty has been vital to preventing the proliferation of nuclear weapons. However, it has been tested by North Korea's withdrawal from it in 2003 and by other nations such as India and Pakistan acquiring nuclear status.

# SALT 1, 1972

*The Strategic Arms Limitation Talks were the first concrete steps taken to control and reduce the arms race.*

## What was SALT 1?

The Strategic Arms Limitation Treaty, or SALT 1, was an agreement between the superpowers to limit their number of nuclear weapons.

## When was SALT 1 signed?

SALT 1 was signed on 26th May, 1972.

## Who signed SALT 1?

The SALT 1 agreement was signed between Richard Nixon and Leonid Brezhnev.

## What was agreed in SALT 1?

There were 4 important agreements in SALT 1:

- The Anti-Ballistic Missile Treaty: anti-ballistic missiles (ABMs) were allowed at only two sites, with 100 missiles at each.
- The Interim Treaty: limited the number of intercontinental ballistic missiles (ICBMs) and submarine launched cruise missiles (SLBMs) the USA and USSR could have. The USA was allowed 1054 ICBMs, and the USSR 1618.
- There would be a five-year delay in building more missiles, so another treaty (SALT 2) would have to be negotiated at the end of that time.
- The Basic Principles Agreement: established what the USA and USSR would do to avoid nuclear war breaking out and the rules if it did occur.

## What were the limitations of SALT 1?

SALT 1 was limited in 3 main ways because:

- It did not cover intermediate-range nuclear weapons, which were still being deployed by both countries.
- It did not include multiple independently targeted reentry vehicles (MIRVs) which carried multiple warheads on a single missile.
- Although it slowed down the arms race, both sides still had enough nuclear missiles to destroy the planet and there was no agreement to not use those missiles.

## Why was SALT 1 important?

SALT 1 was important because of 3 key reasons:

- ✅ It slowed the arms race.
- ✅ It showed an improvement in relations between the USA and the Soviet Union.
- ✅ It led to further improvements such as the Helsinki Conference in 1975 and the SALT 2 negotiations.

> **DID YOU KNOW?**
>
> Gerard Smith was the lead US negotiator at the Strategic Arms Limitation Talks.
>
> His opening comment was: 'The limitation of strategic arms is in the mutual interests of our country and the Soviet Union.'

# PRIME MINISTER ATTLEE

*Clement Attlee was the Prime Minister of Great Britain from 1945 to 1951.*

### Who was Clement Attlee?

Clement Attlee was a Labour politician who served as prime minister of the United Kingdom from 1945 to 1951.

### What were Clement Attlee's beliefs?

Attlee had left-wing beliefs and his government is most famous for creating the NHS. Attlee supported the Marshall Plan *(p.28)* and promoted a NATO *(p.34)* military alliance against the USSR and its satellite states.

### What conferences did Clement Attlee attend?

Attlee attended the Potsdam Conference *(p.22)* in July 1945, to discuss Nazi Germany and how to end the war.

> **DID YOU KNOW?**
>
> Attlee trained as a lawyer, fought in the First World War, and was the founding father of the NHS.

# FULGENCIO BATISTA

*Fulgencio Batista was nicknamed 'El Hombre', or 'The Man'.*

### Who was Batista?

Fulgencio Batista was the American-backed dictator of Cuba from 1952 to 1959, until he was overthrown by Fidel Castro in the Cuban Revolution *(p.51)*.

> **DID YOU KNOW?**
>
> After the Cuban Revolution, Batista lived in exile in various places, including Spain and Portugal.

# LEONID BREZHNEV

*Leonid Brezhnev was the fourth leader of the USSR.*

### Who was Leonid Brezhnev?
Leonid Brezhnev was the fifth leader of the Soviet Union from 1964 until his death in 1982.

### What was the doctrine Brezhnev used?
The Brezhnev Doctrine *(p.59)* was established in 1968. This stated that the actions of an individual communist country affected all communist countries, therefore others must take action to ensure the survival of the regime.

### What was Brezhnev's reaction to Reagan's Zero Option proposal?
Brezhnev rejected President Reagan's Zero Option proposal in November 1981, in which Reagan offered to cancel the deployment of intermediate-range missiles in Europe if the USSR dismantled theirs.

> **DID YOU KNOW?**
> Brezhnev's rule of the USSR was marked by stagnation and corruption.

# PRESIDENT JIMMY CARTER

*President Carter was a member of the Democratic Party.*

### Who was President Carter?
Jimmy Carter was the 39th President of the United States from 1977 to 1981.

### What were President Carter's thoughts on the USSR?
Carter was shocked by the Soviet invasion of Afghanistan and released a statement known as the Carter Doctrine. This stated he would not allow the USSR to control the Middle East.

> **DID YOU KNOW?**
> President Carter was awarded a Nobel Peace Prize in 2002 for his 'decades of untiring effort to find peaceful solutions to international conflicts, to advance democracy and human rights, and to promote economic and social development'.

# PRIME MINISTER CHURCHILL

*Prime Minister Churchill led Great Britain during the Second World War.*

### Who was Winston Churchill?

Sir Winston Churchill was Prime Minister of the United Kingdom from 1940 to 1945, and again from 1951 to 1955.

### What were Churchill's beliefs?

Churchill was a conservative with traditional values. He strongly valued democracy, was in favour of empire, and was incredibly suspicious of Stalin.

### What conferences did Churchill attend?

Churchill attended the Tehran and Yalta conferences to discuss Nazi Germany and how to end the war.

### What was Churchill's 'Iron Curtain' speech?

In March 1946, Churchill made a speech in the USA that criticised the USSR and called it a threat to world peace. Stalin thought this reflected America's beliefs. This speech is referred to as the 'Iron Curtain' speech *(p.26)*.

### What was Churchill's views on the policy of appeasement?

Winston Churchill was an opponent of appeasement, describing it as 'an unmitigated disaster'. Churchill told Britain and France they would have to choose between war and dishonour, and that Hitler was not done expanding the Third Reich.

---

**DID YOU KNOW?**

**Churchill lost the general election to Attlee in July 1945.**
Churchill actually attended the Potsdam Conference but was replaced by Attlee as the new Prime Minister.

---

# PRESIDENT EISENHOWER

*There were several key events relating to the Cold War when President Eisenhower was in power. These included the Korean War, the creation of the Warsaw Pact, Khrushchev's 'Secret Speech', and the U2 spy plane incident.*

### Who was President Eisenhower?

Dwight D Eisenhower was the 34th President of the United States.

### When was Eisenhower president?

Eisenhower was President of the United States from 1953 until 1961.

### What was President Eisenhower's background?

President Eisenhower's background included the following:

- ✓ Eisenhower was a member of the US armed forces throughout the 1920s and 1930s.
- ✓ He was a general in the army during the Second World War and was in charge of the D-Day landings in 1944.

- ✓ He became the supreme commander of NATO *(p.34)* in December 1950.
- ✓ His war record helped him secure the presidency.

### What were the key events of Eisenhower's presidency?

Some of the key events of Eisenhower's presidency included:

- ✓ In 1953 he helped negotiate an armistice that brought peace to Korea.
- ✓ He committed the USA to protecting South Vietnam from communism in 1953.
- ✓ He was in power during the Montgomery Bus Boycott, led by Rosa Parks, which lasted for twelve months between 1955 and 1956.
- ✓ In 1957 he signed the Civil Rights Act and set up a permanent Civil Rights Commission.

### What were Eisenhower's beliefs about the Cold War?

Eisenhower was anti-communist and committed to the policy of containment. He articulated the concept of the 'Domino Theory'.

### What uprising was Eisenhower involved in?

Eisenhower managed to increase tensions between the East and the West when he refused to send US troops to help the Hungarian Uprisings. This led to Eastern Bloc countries realising the West would not support them.

### Did Eisenhower send a spy to the USSR?

In 1960, Khrushchev walked out of a meeting after Eisenhower refused to apologise for sending a U2 spy plane to spy on the Soviet Union.

### What actions did Eisenhower take on civil rights?

Eisenhower took 3 key actions related to civil rights:

- ✓ He introduced the Civil Rights Act of 1957 that sought to ensure all African Americans could register to vote.
- ✓ Following the ruling in the case of Brown v Board of Education, Eisenhower did not want to use his powers to support the rapid desegregation of schools as he believed it should proceed slowly.
- ✓ He sent federal troops to Little Rock to protect the African American students and enforce integration.

---

**DID YOU KNOW?**

**President Eisenhower gave a speech after Stalin died called 'Chance for Peace'.**
In that speech, he called on the USSR to work for peace.

---

# GEORGE KENNAN

*George F Kennan was a historian and a diplomat.*

### Who was George Kennan?

George Kennan was an American diplomat and the US ambassador in Moscow.

### What were Kennan's beliefs?
Kennan was a strong advocate of the US policy of containment and was suspicious of the Soviet Union.

### What telegram did Kennan send?
In 1946, Kennan sent the 'Long Telegram *(p.24)*' to Truman. This reported hostile attitudes in Moscow towards the USA and said Stalin wanted to destroy capitalism.

> **DID YOU KNOW?**
> It was Kennan's telegram, named after him, which coined the phrase 'containment'. This then became the heart of the Truman Doctrine.

# PRESIDENT JOHN F KENNEDY
*I take pride in the words, Ich bin ein Berliner' - JFK during his visit to Berlin*

### Who was President Kennedy?
John F Kennedy, commonly referred to as JFK, was the 35th President of the United States.

### When was Kennedy president?
John F Kennedy was president between January 1961 and November 1963.

### What was Kennedy's background?
Kennedy's background included the following:
- He came from an Irish-American family which was very wealthy and heavily involved in politics.
- He went to Harvard University and studied politics. He wrote his dissertation on Britain's policy of the appeasement of Adolf Hitler.
- He was in the US navy and served in the Second World War, where he was seriously injured when his boat was destroyed by the Japanese.

### What were the key events of Kennedy's presidency?
The key events of Kennedy's presidency included the following:
- Kennedy created the Peace Corps in 1961.
- The Bay of Pigs Invasion in Cuba, in April 1961.
- In May 1961 he pledged America would put a man on the moon by the end of the decade.
- The Berlin Wall *(p.50)* was built in 1961.
- The Cuban Missile Crisis *(p.54)* took place in October 1962.
- He signed the Limited Nuclear Test Ban Treaty in August 1963.

### What were Kennedy's beliefs about the Cold War?
Kennedy was anti-communist and, like his predecessors, was committed to containing communism. However, he was aware of the dangers of nuclear warfare after tensions were brought to the brink during the Cuban Missile Crisis *(p.54)*, and wanted to reduce the chances of nuclear war.

### What was President Kennedy's role in the Bay of Pigs invasion?
Kennedy attempted to implement a counter-revolution in Cuba by sending in Cuban exiles. The aim was to make it look like the USA wasn't involved. However, the plan failed.

### What was President Kennedy's involvement with the Cuban Missile Crisis?
In 1962, two U2 spy planes spotted what looked like missiles in Cuba. This led to a tense 13 days where Kennedy deliberated what to do. He decided to set up a naval blockade and managed to prevent nuclear war.

### What was President Kennedy's role in Vietnam?
President Kennedy continued to support South Vietnam with money, military advisers and commandos.

### How did President Kennedy die?
Kennedy was assassinated in November 1963 in Dallas, Texas.

### Why was President Kennedy in Dallas?
Kennedy was in Dallas because he needed to win support from the southern Democrats, nicknamed the Dixiecrats, for his Civil Rights bill.

> **DID YOU KNOW?**
> The Kennedy family was rich and powerful.
> JFK's brothers, Robert and Ted, both became famous senators.

# NIKITA KHRUSHCHEV
*Nikita Khrushchev was the third leader of the USSR.*

### Who was Khrushchev?
Nikita Khrushchev led the Soviet Union after Stalin's death up until 1964.

### What was Khrushchev's speech?
Khrushchev openly criticised Stalin in his 'Secret Speech' in 1956. Khrushchev began to de-Stalinise the Soviet Union and said he wanted a peaceful co-existence with the West. People hoped this would end the Cold War *(p.14)*.

### How did tensions increase under Khrushchev?
The Hungarian Uprising *(p.47)* managed to increase international tensions as countries in eastern Europe began to realise the USA would not help them.

> **DID YOU KNOW?**
>
> **Khrushchev was the son of a Ukrainian peasant.**
> He was not well educated but rose through the ranks of the Communist Party. Despite his criticism of Stalin's brutality in his 'Secret Speech', he was involved in the Great Purges of the 1930s.

# GEORGE MARSHALL

*George C Marshall had a long military career and was partly responsible for the Normandy invasion of 1944.*

### Who was Marshall?

George C Marshall was a general in the American army and statesman. He served as Secretary of State and Secretary of Defense under President Truman.

### What plan did George Marshall come up with?

The Marshall Plan *(p.28)* aimed to provide economic aid to war-torn countries in Europe. The purpose of this was keep them tied to the USA instead of falling to communism.

> **DID YOU KNOW?**
>
> George C Marshall was awarded the Nobel Peace Prize in 1953 for creating the Marshall Plan.

# IMRE NAGY

*Imre Nagy was a life-long member of the Communist Party.*

### Who was Imre Nagy?

Imre Nagy was a Hungarian communist politician who served as Prime Minister from 1953 to 1955 and again during the Hungarian Uprising *(p.47)* in 1956.

### What uprising was Nagy involved in?

Nagy introduced reforms that Khrushchev accepted. However, Nagy then announced that Hungary was leaving the Warsaw Pact *(p.35)*, so Khrushchev sent in the Red Army.

### How did Nagy die?

As a result of the Hungarian Uprising *(p.47)*, Nagy was executed.

> **DID YOU KNOW?**
>
> Nagy was executed by hanging in 1958.

# NIKOLAI NOVIKOV

*Nikolai Novikov's telegram greatly influenced Stalin's attitudes towards the USA.*

### Who was Nikolai Novikov?

Nikolai Novikov was a Soviet diplomat and the USSR's ambassador in Washington.

### What was Novikov's telegram?

Stalin received a telegram from Novikov which reported that America wanted to dominate the world and was preparing for war with the USSR.

# ANTONIN NOVOTNÝ

*Antonin Novotný was hard-line Stalinist.*

### Who was Novotný?

Antonin Novotný was the communist Prime Minister of Czechoslovakia from 1957 to 1968.

### What important events occurred while Novotný was leader?

Novotný was leader when the Prague Spring *(p.56)* began, where people tried to reform the communist system in Czechoslovakia to create 'socialism with a human face'.

> **DID YOU KNOW?**
>
> Novotný was allowed to re-join the Central Committee of the Czechoslovakian Communist Party after the Prague Spring, but he never regained his power.

# PRESIDENT ROOSEVELT

*President Roosevelt played a key role in two of the three wartime meetings of the Grand Alliance.*

### What were President Roosevelt's beliefs during the Second World War?

President Roosevelt strongly believed in democracy. However, he formed an alliance with the USSR to protect the USA against Japan. He believed Stalin could be 'managed' and remain a post-war ally.

*Get our free app at GCSEHistory.com*

### What conferences did Roosevelt attend at the end of the Second World War to discuss his ideas?
President Roosevelt attended the Tehran and Yalta conferences, which discussed Nazi Germany and how to end the war.

> **DID YOU KNOW?**
> President Roosevelt was awarded the Nobel Peace Prize in 1906 for his role in the negotiations for the Treaty of Portsmouth that ended the Russo-Japanese War of 1904-05.

# PRESIDENT HARRY TRUMAN

*'I believe that it must be the policy of the United States to support free peoples who are resisting attempted subjugation by armed minorities or by outside pressures.' - President Truman*

### Who was President Truman?
Harry S Truman was the 33rd President of the United States, holding office from 1945 to 1953.

### What was an overview of Truman's time as president?
Truman's time as president included the following events:
- He took over from Franklin D Roosevelt during the Second World War.
- He oversaw huge challenges both domestically and internationally as America transitioned from fighting the Second World War in 1945 to the onset of the Cold War (p.14) between 1947 and 1949.
- His policy of the Truman Doctrine (p.27) and the policy of the containment became the cornerstone of American foreign policy for decades.
- In the years after his presidency he faced huge criticism as the president who 'lost China to communism'.
- He is now considered by historians to be one of America's greatest presidents.

### What was President Truman's attitude towards communism?
Truman objected to the USSR's control over the countries of eastern Europe. He believed the USSR was determined to expand, so he sought to contain the spread of communism during his time in office.

### What conferences did Truman attend?
Truman attended the Potsdam Conference (p.22) in July 1945 to discuss Nazi Germany and how to end the war.

### What was Truman's involvement in the Cold War?
The Truman Doctrine (p.27), in 1947, highlighted America's new stance on communism, and signalled the beginning of the US policy of containment.

> **DID YOU KNOW?**
> **Harry S Truman's middle name was, literally, 'S'.**
> It was included to honour his grandfathers, who both had 'S' in their names.

# GLOSSARY

## A

Aggression - angry, hostile or violent behaviour displayed without provocation.

Agricultural - relating to agriculture.

Alliance - a union between groups or countries that benefits each member.

Allies - parties working together for a common objective, such as countries involved in a war. In both world wars, 'Allies' refers to those countries on the side of Great Britain.

Ambassador - someone, often a diplomat, who represents their state, country or organisation in a different setting or place.

Armistice - an agreement between two or more opposing sides in a war to stop fighting.

Artillery - large guns used in warfare.

Assassinate - to murder someone, usually an important figure, often for religious or political reasons.

## B

Blockade - a way of blocking or sealing an area to prevent goods, supplies or people from entering or leaving. It often refers to blocking transport routes.

Boycott - a way of protesting or bringing about change by refusing to buy something or use services.

Brinkmanship - pushing a disagreement to its limits in the hope the other side backs down, especially pertaining to war.

Buffer - a protective barrier.

Buffer zone - a neutral area of land to separate hostile forces or nations and provide protection. In the Cold War, Eastern Europe was the buffer zone between Western Europe and the USSR.

## C

Cabinet - politically, the group of senior ministers responsible for controlling government policy.

Campaign - a political movement to get something changed; in military terms, it refers to a series of operations to achieve a goal.

Capitalism - the idea of goods and services being exchanged for money, private ownership of property and businesses, and acceptance of a hierarchical society.

Censorship - the control of information in the media by a government, whereby information considered obscene or unacceptable is suppressed.

Chancellor - a senior state official who, in some countries, is the head of the government and responsible for the day-to-day running of the nation.

Civil rights - the rights a citizen has to political or social freedoms, such as the right to vote or freedom of speech.

Civilian - a non-military person.

Claim - someone's assertion of their right to something - for example, a claim to the throne.

Coalition government - a government formed by more than one political party.

Coalition, Coalitions - a temporary alliance, such as when a group of countries fights together.

Coexistence - living or existing together at the same time or in the same place.

Collective security - a policy adopted by the League of Nations, with the idea members should feel safe from attack as all nations agreed to defend each other.

Colonialism - when a country seeks to bring other territories under its control, often with the aim of dominating its economy. Religion and cultural practices may also be imposed.

Communism - the belief, based on the ideas of Karl Marx, that all people should be equal in society without government, money or private property. Everything is owned by by the people, and each person receives according to need.

Communist - a believer in communism.

Conference - a formal meeting to discuss common issues of interest or concern.

Conscription - mandatory enlistment of people into a state service, usually the military.

Conservative - someone who dislikes change and prefers traditional values. It can also refer to a member of the Conservative Party.

Consolidate - to strengthen a position, often politically, by bringing several things together into a more effective whole.

Constitution - rules, laws or principles that set out how a country is governed.

Containment - meaning to keep something under control or within limits, it often refers to the American idea of stopping the spread of communism.

Cooperate, Cooperation - to work together to achieve a common aim. Frequently used in relation to politics, economics or law.

Council - an advisory or administrative body set up to manage the affairs of a place or organisation. The Council of the League of Nations contained the organisation's most powerful members.

Counter-attack - an attack made in response to one by an opponent.

Currency - an umbrella term for any form of legal tender, but most commonly referring to money.

## D

Deadlock - a situation where no action can be taken and neither side can make progress against the other; effectively a draw.

Defect - the act of defection; to leave your country or cause for another.

Demilitarised - to remove all military forces from an area and forbid them to be stationed there.

# GLOSSARY

Democracy - a political system where a population votes for its government on a regular basis. The word is Greek for 'the rule of people' or 'people power'.

Democratic - relating to or supporting the principles of democracy.

Deploy - to move military troops or equipment into position or a place so they are ready for action.

Deport - to expel someone from a country and, usually, return them to their homeland.

Desegregation - a policy of removing racial segregation (separation).

Deterrent - something that discourages an action or behaviour.

Dictator - a ruler with absolute power over a country, often acquired by force.

Dictatorship - a form of government where an individual or small group has total power, ruling without tolerance for other views or opposition.

Disarmament - the reduction or removal of weaponry.

Dispute - a disagreement or argument; often used to describe conflict between different countries.

Dissent, Dissenting - to hold or express views against an idea or policy, often in politics.

Doctrine - a stated principle of government policy; can also refer to a set of beliefs held and taught by a church, political party or other group.

Dollar imperialism - a phrase used by the Soviet Union's Foreign Minister, Molotov, in accusing the USA of using its economic strength to take over Europe through the Marshall Plan.

Détente - the easing of tension, especially between two countries.

## E

Economic - relating to the economy; also used when justifying something in terms of profitability.

Economy - a country, state or region's position in terms of production and consumption of goods and services, and the supply of money.

Embassy - historically, a deputation sent by one ruler, state or country to another. More recently, it is also the accepted name for the official residence or offices of an ambassador.

Empire - a group of states or countries ruled over and controlled by a single monarch.

Exile - to be banned from one's original country, usually as a punishment or for political reasons.

## F

Fascist - one who believes in fascism.

Federal - in US politics this means 'national', referring to the whole country rather than any individual state.

Foreign policy - a government's strategy for dealing with other nations.

Free elections - elections in which voters are free to vote without interference.

Front - in war, the area where fighting is taking place.

Frontier - a line or border between two areas.

## H

Hard line - strict and uncompromising.

## I

Ideology - a set of ideas and ideals, particularly around political ideas or economic policy, often shared by a group of people.

Import - to bring goods or services into a different country to sell.

Independence, Independent - to be free of control, often meaning by another country, allowing the people of a nation the ability to govern themselves.

Industrial - related to industry, manufacturing and/or production

Industry - the part of the economy concerned with turning raw materials into into manufactured goods, for example making furniture from wood.

Intercontinental ballistic missile - a guided ballistic missile with a minimum range of 5,500km or 3,400 miles.

International relations - the relationships between different countries.

Iron Curtain - a phrase used by Winston Churchill to describe the non-physical divide created by Stalin between Eastern Europe and the West.

## L

Legitimacy, Legitimate - accepted by law or conforming to the rules; can be defended as valid.

Liberal - politically, someone who believes in allowing personal freedom without too much control by the government or state.

## M

Merchant ships - unarmed ships used for carrying supplies and goods.

Military force - the use of armed forces.

Minister - a senior member of government, usually responsible for a particular area such as education or finance.

Monarchists - people in favour of living in a country governed by a monarchy.

## N

Nationalism, Nationalist, Nationalistic - identifying with your own nation and supporting its interests, often to the detriment or exclusion of other nations.

# GLOSSARY

## O

Offensive - another way of saying an attack or campaign.

## P

Parliament - a group of politicians who make the laws of their country, usually elected by the population.

Peasant - a poor farmer.

Population - the number of people who live in a specified place.

Poverty - the state of being extremely poor.

Predecessor - the person who came before; the previous person to fill a role or position.

President - the elected head of state of a republic.

Prevent, Preventative, Preventive - steps taken to stop something from happening.

Production - a term used to describe how much of something is made, for example saying a factory has a high production rate.

Propaganda - biased information aimed at persuading people to think a certain way.

Prosecute - to institute or conduct legal proceedings against a person or organisation.

Proxy war - a conflict between two sides acting on behalf of other parties who are not directly involved, but who have usually supplied equipment, arms and/or money.

## Q

Quarantine - a period of isolation where a person or animal who has or may have a communicable disease is kept away from others.

## R

Rebellion - armed resistance against a government or leader, or resistance to other authority or control.

Rebels - people who rise in opposition or armed resistance against an established government or leader.

Reform, Reforming - change, usually in order to improve an institution or practice.

Refugee, Refugees - a person who has been forced to leave where they live due to war, disaster or persecution.

Reparations - payments made by the defeated countries in a war to the victors to help pay for the cost of and damage from the fighting.

Repressive - a harsh or authoritarian action; usually used to describe governmental abuse of power.

Revolution - the forced overthrow of a government or social system by its own people.

Rig, Rigged - politically, to interfere in or fix an election to determine the winner.

Riots - violent disturbances involving a crowd of people.

## S

Sanctions - actions taken against states who break international laws, such as a refusal to trade with them or supply necessary commodities.

Satellite state - a country under the control of another, such as countries under USSR control during the Cold War.

Sino - is a a reference to China or something relating to China. It is a prefix which is used instead of China.

Socialism - a political and economic system where most resources, such as factories and businesses, are owned by the state or workers with the aim of achieving greater equality between rich and poor.

Soviet - an elected workers' council at local, regional or national level in the former Soviet Union. It can also be a reference to the Soviet Union or the USSR.

Sphere of influence - an area or country under the influence of another country.

Stalemate - a situation where no action can be taken and neither side can make progress against the other; effectively a draw.

Standard of living - level of wealth and goods available to an individual or group.

State, States - an area of land or a territory ruled by one government.

Strike - a refusal by employees to work as a form of protest, usually to bring about change in their working conditions. It puts pressure on their employer, who cannot run the business without workers.

Summit - a formal meeting between two or more heads of government.

Superior - better or higher in rank, status or quality.

## T

Tactic - a strategy or method of achieving a goal.

Terrain - a stretch of land and usually used to refer to its physical features, eg mountainous, jungle etc.

Territories, Territory - an area of land under the control of a ruler/country.

Thaw - the period of time where the relationship between the USSR and the USA improved.

Treaty - a formal agreement, signed and ratified by two or more parties.

Tsar - the Russian word for emperor; can also be spelled 'czar'.

## U

Ultimatum - a final demand, with the threat of consequences if it is not met.

# GLOSSARY

## V

Veto - the right to reject a decision or proposal.

## W

Western powers - a group term used to describe developed capitalist nations, such as Britain and the USA.

# INDEX

## A
American intervention in Korea - 44
Arms Race - 36
Atomic Bomb - 23
Attlee, Clement - 66

## B
Batista, Fulgencio - 66
Bay of Pigs - 53
Berlin Airlift - 32
Berlin Blockade - 31
Berlin Crisis - 49
Berlin Wall - 50
Brezhnev Doctrine - 59
Brezhnev, Leonid - 67

## C
China and Détente - 61
Churchill, Winston - 68
Civil War, Russian - 16
Cold War - 14
Cold War, Russian Revolution - 15
Comecon - 30
Cominform - 29
Conference of Tehran - 19
Cuban Missile Crisis - 54
Cuban Revolution - 51

## D
De-Stalinisation - 46
Division of Germany - 33
Dubček, Alexander - 58
Détente - 60

## E
Eisenhower, Dwight D - 68

## F
FDR, the Second World War - 73

## G
General MacArthur and the Korean War - 43
Grand Alliance - 18

## H
Hotline - 62
Hungarian Uprising - 47

## I
Iron Curtain Speech - 26

## K
Kennan, George - 69
Kennedy, President - 70
Khrushchev, Nikita - 71
Korean Invasion - 41
Korean War - 37

## L
Limited Test Ban Treaty - 63
Long Telegram - 24

## M
MacArthur, General, and the Korean War - 43
Marshall Plan - 28
Marshall, George - 72

## N
NATO - 34
Nagy, Imre - 72
Non-Proliferation of Nuclear Weapons Treaty - 64
Novikov Telegram - 25
Novikov, Nikolai - 73
Novotny, Antonin - 73

## O
Outer Space Treaty - 64

## P
Peaceful Coexistence - 45
Potsdam Conference - 22
Prague Spring - 56
President Carter doctrine - 67

## R
Roosevelt, the Second World War - 73
Russian Civil War - 16

# INDEX

Russian Revolution and the Cold War - *15*

## S

Soviet Satellite States - *25*

Strategic Arms Limitation Treaty I - *65*

## T

Tehran Conference - *19*

Truman Doctrine - *27*

Truman, Harry - *74*

## U

U2 Crisis - *52*

USA and the invasion of South Korea - *42*

## W

Warsaw Pact - *35*

## Y

Yalta Conference - *20*